I0623639

VEGETARIAN

BARNES
& NOBLE
BOOKS

NEW YORK

Pictured on front cover:

Herbed Pasta Primavera, *page 12*

Previously published as
Better Homes and Gardens® Cooking for Today Vegetarian Recipes

Copyright © 2004, 1993 by Meredith Corporation, Des Moines, Iowa. First Edition.

This edition published for Barnes & Noble, Inc., by Meredith Books.

All rights reserved. No part of this book may be used or reproduced in any
manner whatsoever without the written permission of the Publisher.

Printed in China

ISBN: 0-7607-6041-1

Never before have so many Americans chosen to forego meat in favor of meatless dining—and for good reasons. Vegetarianism has been associated with heart healthiness for years, thanks to a diet that's low in fat and cholesterol. But what does it mean to be a vegetarian? Take your pick. Vegetarians run the gamut from strict vegetarians who never eat a morsel of meat, fish, fowl, or dairy products to semi-vegetarians who simply eat less meat and more vegetables. No matter where you fit in, going meatless makes good nutritional sense. In fact, a meatless main dish can offer you a valuable mix of nutrients with lots of variety, taste, and visual appeal. All at a very affordable price, too.

On the following pages you will find must-try main dishes such as Fresh Vegetable Risotto and Cheese and Basil Polenta with Tomato-Basil Sauce, hearty soups such as Spicy Black Bean Chili and Creamy Two-Bean Chowder with Pesto, meal-maker salads such as Pasta-Millet Salad with Porcini Mushrooms and Sizzling Goat Cheese Salad, and sensational sandwiches such as Grilled Brie Sandwiches with Greens and Asparagus Egg Salad with Dill Dressing. So whether you're a strict vegetarian or just like to go meatless occasionally, you'll savor the sensational recipes in this book since we eliminated the meat but not the gusto.

CONTENTS

MIX-AND-MATCH PROTEIN

Some say it's a challenge to incorporate enough protein into meatless meals. But it's easy if you follow a few simple rules. Just remember to use the right combination of nuts and seeds, legumes, grains, and dairy products.

The best marriages for making complete proteins are grains and legumes, legumes and seeds, and grains and dairy. Keep these simple mergers in mind and you'll be on your way to protein-packed meatless meals.

LIGHT AND LEAN DAIRY PRODUCTS

Dairy foods can play a major role in meatless main dishes, but unfortunately many of them contain a high amount of fat and calories. You can make smart dairy choices without tipping the fat and calorie scales. Among some of your healthiest choices are skim milk, nonfat and low-fat yogurt, nonfat and "light" sour cream, reduced-fat hard cheeses, and low-fat cottage cheese.

BEAN BASICS

Using canned beans in many of the recipes can save you time, but they can also contribute sodium to your diet. A simple solution to this salty situation is to rinse the beans in a colander under running water and let them drain. You'll still have great tasting beans but none of the salty liquid that comes with them. Or, if you want to eliminate all the added sodium from beans, use dry beans and prepare them yourself. Here's how. In a Dutch oven combine 1 pound rinsed beans and 8 cups cold water. Bring to a boil; reduce heat. Simmer for 2 minutes. Remove from heat. Cover and let stand for 1 hour. (Or, omit simmering; soak beans in cold water overnight in covered pan.) Drain and rinse. Combine beans and 8 cups fresh water. Bring to a boil; reduce heat. Cover and simmer for 1 to 2 hours or till tender, stirring occasionally. (Cooked beans can be drained, cooled, and frozen for up to 2 months for use in future recipes.)

Tofu Trivia

In the beginning there was just tofu. Plain, simple, and nutritious. But thanks to its growing popularity, there are more kinds of tofu on the market, making it harder for the average consumer to choose the right one. Here's a simple guide to the types of tofu you can find at your supermarket:

■ Silken tofu is a Japanese style of tofu with the softest texture of all. This delicate texture makes it ideal for soups and sauces.

■ Chinese tofu is firmer than silken tofu but is still smooth and creamy. Use it in soups and simmered recipes.

■ Regular Chinese or Japanese tofu is pressed longer than silken or Chinese tofu to remove more water, giving it a firmer texture. Use it the same as soft tofu as well as in casseroles and stir-fry dishes.

■ Firm and extra-firm tofu contains less water than other types of tofu. It also has a somewhat grainy texture and would be a good choice for stir-frying or recipes where you want the tofu to remain intact.

Recipe Facts and Figures

Thanks to computer software, we can provide you with a wealth of nutrition information for each recipe in the book. You'll find the basics such as the number of calories and grams of protein for each serving plus a few extras such as fiber content and percentage of calories from fat. In the process, we assumed the following:

■ Garnishes and optional ingredients were omitted from the nutrition analysis.

■ Ingredients with a weight range or amount range ($\frac{1}{4}$ to $\frac{1}{2}$ teaspoon, for example) were analyzed at the lesser weight or amount.

■ Where you find two ingredient options to pick from (cilantro or parsley, for example), the first was used in the nutrition rundown.

Broth Math

Many of the recipes in this book call for vegetable broth, chicken broth, or beef broth. If you are fresh out of canned broth, you can use bouillon granules or cubes as an easy substitute. Just remember that 1 cup of canned broth is equivalent to 1 teaspoon of granules or 1 cube dissolved in 1 cup water.

VEGETABLE LASAGNA

If you like, substitute 1 cup chopped fresh mushrooms for the dried mushrooms. Simply cook the fresh mushrooms with the onion, green pepper, and carrots and use water instead of the dried mushroom liquid.

8 ounces lasagna noodles (9 noodles)
½ cup (½ ounce) dried porcini or shiitake mushrooms
1 cup boiling water
1 large onion, chopped (1 cup)
1 large green pepper, chopped (1 cup)
2 medium carrots, chopped (1 cup)
4 cloves garlic, minced
2 tablespoons margarine *or* butter
4 cups chopped broccoli (flowerets and stems)
1 15-ounce container ricotta cheese
1 cup shredded mozzarella cheese (4 ounces)
½ cup grated Parmesan *or* Romano cheese
2 eggs
¼ cup snipped parsley
½ teaspoon dried thyme, crushed
½ teaspoon dried marjoram, crushed
¼ teaspoon pepper
1 30½-ounce jar meatless spaghetti sauce
¼ cup grated Parmesan *or* Romano cheese

Cook lasagna noodles according to package directions; drain. Meanwhile, in a medium bowl combine dried mushrooms and boiling water. Let stand for 20 minutes. Drain and squeeze mushrooms, reserving liquid. Remove and discard mushroom stems. Coarsely chop mushrooms. Set aside.

In a large skillet cook onion, green pepper, carrots, and garlic in hot margarine or butter till tender but not brown. Add broccoli and ½ *cup* reserved mushroom liquid. Bring to a boil; reduce heat. Cover and simmer about 5 minutes or till broccoli is just crisp-tender. Stir in mushrooms.

In a medium bowl stir together ricotta cheese, mozzarella cheese, ½ cup Parmesan or Romano cheese, eggs, parsley, thyme, marjoram, and pepper.

In a 3-quart rectangular baking dish evenly spread ½ *cup* of the spaghetti sauce. Arrange *3* lasagna noodles over sauce. Layer with *half* of the cheese mixture, *half* of the vegetable mixture, and *1 cup* of the spaghetti sauce. Repeat layers, ending with noodles. Spoon remaining spaghetti sauce over the top. Sprinkle with ¼ cup Parmesan or Romano cheese.

Cover and bake in a 375° oven for 20 minutes. Uncover and bake about 10 minutes more or till heated through. Makes 8 servings.

Nutrition information per serving: 485 calories, 30 g protein, 54 g carbohydrate, 20 g fat (8 g saturated), 86 mg cholesterol, 979 mg sodium, 891 mg potassium.

HEARTY RICE SKILLET

If you use instant brown rice when preparing this one-dish recipe, use only ⅔ cup water.

1 15-ounce can black, garbanzo, *or* kidney beans, rinsed and drained
1 14½-ounce can stewed tomatoes, cut up
2 cups loose-pack frozen mixed vegetables
1 cup water
¾ cup quick-cooking brown rice
½ teaspoon dried thyme *or* dillweed, crushed
  Several dashes bottled hot pepper sauce (optional)
1 10¾-ounce can condensed tomato soup
⅓ cup slivered almonds, toasted
½ cup shredded mozzarella *or* cheddar cheese (2 ounces)

In a large skillet stir together beans, *undrained* tomatoes, vegetables, water, *uncooked* rice, thyme or dillweed, and, if desired, hot pepper sauce. Bring to a boil; reduce heat. Cover and simmer for 12 to 14 minutes or till rice is tender. Stir in soup; heat through.

Before serving, stir in almonds and sprinkle with cheese. Makes 4 servings.

Nutrition information per serving: 354 calories, 19 g protein, 57 g carbohydrate, 10 g fat (2 g saturated), 8 mg cholesterol, 1,244 mg sodium, 917 mg potassium.

DOUBLE CORN TORTILLA CASSEROLE

The double dose of corn comes from corn tortillas and whole kernel corn. Serve this tangy home-style dish with your favorite salsa or picante sauce.

8   corn tortillas
1½   cups shredded Monterey Jack cheese
        (6 ounces)
1   cup frozen whole kernel corn
4   green onions, sliced (½ cup)
2   eggs
1   cup buttermilk
1   4-ounce can diced green chili peppers

Grease a 2-quart square baking dish. Tear tortillas into bite-size pieces. Arrange *half* of the tortillas in baking dish. Top with *half* of the cheese, *half* of the corn, and *half* of the green onions. Repeat layering with remaining tortillas, cheese, corn, and onions.

Stir together eggs, buttermilk, and chili peppers. Gently pour over tortilla mixture. Bake, uncovered, in a 325° oven about 30 minutes or till a knife inserted near the center comes out clean. Serve warm. Makes 4 servings.

Nutrition information per serving: 388 calories, 21 g protein, 37 g carbohydrate, 18 g fat (9 g saturated), 146 mg cholesterol, 564 mg sodium, 344 mg potassium.

HERBED PASTA PRIMAVERA

For the best flavor, use fresh parsley, fresh basil, and freshly shredded Parmesan cheese.

6 ounces linguine, spaghetti, *or* fettuccine
1 cup water
2 teaspoons cornstarch
2 teaspoons instant vegetable *or* chicken bouillon granules
1 tablespoon olive oil
2 cloves garlic, minced
8 ounces fresh asparagus, cut into 1-inch pieces
2 medium carrots, very thinly bias-sliced (1 cup)
1 medium onion, chopped (½ cup)
1 6-ounce package frozen pea pods, thawed and well drained
⅔ cup sliced almonds *or* chopped cashews
¼ cup snipped parsley *or* 1 tablespoon dried parsley flakes
2 tablespoons snipped fresh basil *or* 1½ teaspoons dried basil, crushed
¼ teaspoon pepper
⅓ cup finely shredded Parmesan cheese

Cook pasta according to package directions; drain. Meanwhile, for sauce, in a small bowl stir together water, cornstarch, and bouillon granules. Set aside.

Pour olive oil into wok or large skillet. Preheat over medium-high heat. Stir-fry garlic in hot oil for 15 seconds. Add asparagus, carrots, and onion; stir fry for 2 minutes. Add pea pods, almonds or cashews, parsley, basil, and pepper. Stir-fry about 1 minute more or till vegetables are crisp-tender. Remove vegetable mixture from wok.

Stir sauce. Add sauce to wok. Cook and stir till thickened and bubbly. Cook and stir 1 minute more. Return vegetable mixture to wok; toss to coat. Heat through.

To serve, spoon vegetable mixture over hot cooked pasta. Sprinkle with Parmesan cheese. Makes 4 servings.

Nutrition information per serving: 432 calories, 17 g protein, 52 g carbohydrate, 19 g fat (3 g saturated), 7 mg cholesterol, 642 mg sodium, 612 mg potassium.

TOFU AND CHEESE-STUFFED SHELLS

No one will ever know that these giant pasta shells contain tofu....unless you tell.

12 jumbo pasta shells
¼ cup shredded carrot
1 green onion, sliced (2 tablespoons)
8 ounces tofu (fresh bean curd), drained
½ cup ricotta cheese
½ cup shredded cheddar cheese (2 ounces)
½ cup shredded mozzarella cheese (2 ounces)
1 egg white
¼ teaspoon salt
¼ teaspoon pepper
1 16-ounce can tomatoes, cut up
½ of a 6-ounce can (⅓ cup) tomato paste
1 teaspoon dried basil, crushed
1 teaspoon dried oregano, crushed
½ teaspoon sugar
¼ teaspoon garlic powder
¼ teaspoon fennel seed, crushed (optional)
Grated Parmesan cheese (optional)

Cook pasta according to package directions; drain. Rinse with cold water. Drain and set aside. Meanwhile, in a small saucepan cook carrot and green onion in a small amount of water till tender; drain.

For filling, in a medium mixing bowl mash tofu with a fork. Stir in carrot mixture, ricotta cheese, cheddar cheese, *¼ cup* of the mozzarella cheese, egg white, salt, and pepper. Set aside.

For sauce, in a medium saucepan combine *undrained* tomatoes, tomato paste, basil, oregano, sugar, garlic powder, and, if desired, fennel seed. Bring to a boil; reduce heat. Simmer, uncovered, for 10 minutes.

Stuff *each* cooked pasta shell with about *1 rounded tablespoon* of the filling. Place shells in an ungreased 2-quart square baking dish. Pour sauce over shells. Cover and bake in a 350° oven about 25 minutes or till heated through. Sprinkle with remaining mozzarella cheese. If desired, serve with Parmesan cheese. Makes 4 servings.

Nutrition information per serving: 318 calories, 21 g protein, 32 g carbohydrate, 13 g fat (6 g saturated), 32 mg cholesterol, 558 mg sodium, 695 mg potassium.

WINTER SQUASH WITH PEARS AND CHEESE

You can make this homey recipe in less than 1 hour by preparing the nutty ricotta filling while the acorn squash bake.

2   medium acorn squash
2   medium pears, cored and chopped
      (2 cups)
4   green onions, sliced (½ cup)
1   clove garlic, minced
1   tablespoon cooking oil
1   15-ounce container ricotta cheese
½   cup shredded cheddar cheese
      (2 ounces)
¼   cup raisins
¼   cup pine nuts *or* chopped pecans
1   teaspoon finely shredded lemon peel
¼   teaspoon ground nutmeg
¼   teaspoon salt
⅛   teaspoon pepper

Halve squash lengthwise; remove seeds. Place squash, cut side down, in a 2-quart rectangular baking dish. Bake, uncovered, in a 350° oven about 30 minutes or till tender.

Meanwhile, in a large skillet cook pears, green onions, and garlic in hot oil till tender but not brown. Remove from heat. Stir in ricotta cheese, cheddar cheese, raisins, pine nuts or pecans, lemon peel, and nutmeg. Turn squash, cut side up, in baking dish. Season with salt and pepper. Spoon cheese mixture into the baked squash, mounding as necessary. Continue baking for 20 to 25 minutes more or till heated through. Makes 4 servings.

Nutrition information per serving: 428 calories, 20 g protein, 44 g carbohydrate, 22 g fat (10 g saturated), 48 mg cholesterol, 362 mg sodium, 848 mg potassium.

FRESH TOMATO PIZZA WITH PESTO

For best results, make this recipe when ripe, juicy summer tomatoes are at their peak.

½ cup purchased pesto *or* Homemade
    Pesto (see recipe, page 139)
1 16-ounce prebaked Italian bread shell
3 medium ripe tomatoes, thinly sliced
    Freshly ground pepper
1   2¼-ounce can sliced pitted ripe
    olives, drained (scant ⅔ cup)
2 cups shredded Monterey Jack *or*
    mozzarella cheese (8 ounces)

Spread pesto evenly over bread shell. Place on large pizza pan or baking dish. Arrange tomato slices on top. Season with pepper. Sprinkle with olives and Monterey Jack or mozzarella cheese. Bake in a 425° oven for 10 to 15 minutes or till cheese melts and tomatoes are warm. Cut into wedges. Makes 4 servings.

Nutrition information per serving: 776 calories, 32 g protein, 60 g carbohydrate, 48 g fat (11 g saturated), 60 mg cholesterol, 1,265 mg sodium, 255 mg potassium.

PIZZA CRUST CAPER

If a prebaked Italian bread shell is unavailable for pizza making, you can use a 10-ounce package of refrigerated pizza dough instead. Simply unroll the dough onto a greased 12-inch pizza pan, building up the edges slightly. Bake in a 425° oven for 8 minutes. If necessary, cover the edges of the dough with foil to prevent overbrowning. Proceed as directed in the recipes for Fresh Tomato Pizza with Pesto and Nutty Endive Pizza with Two Cheeses (see recipe, page 21).

NUTTY ENDIVE PIZZA WITH TWO CHEESES

Curly endive is a salad green with frilly, narrow, dark green leaves that curl at the edges. This prickly green adds a pleasantly mild bitter taste to the pizza.

1   small red onion, chopped (⅓ cup)
2   cloves garlic, minced
1   tablespoon walnut oil *or* olive oil
4   cups torn curly endive *or* spinach
¼   teaspoon crushed red pepper
1   16-ounce prebaked Italian bread shell
1   cup shredded Swiss cheese (4 ounces)
¼   cup pine nuts *or* coarsely chopped
      walnuts, toasted
1   cup shredded Colby cheese (4 ounces)

In a medium skillet cook red onion and garlic in hot oil till tender but not brown. Add the endive or spinach and crushed red pepper. Cover and cook over low heat for 2 minutes.

Place bread shell on a 12-inch pizza pan or large baking sheet. Sprinkle Swiss cheese evenly over bread shell. Top with endive mixture and toasted nuts. Sprinkle Colby cheese over the top. Bake in a 425° oven about 10 minutes or till cheese melts. Cut into wedges. Makes 4 servings.

Nutrition information per serving: 616 calories, 31 g protein, 56 g carbohydrate, 32 g fat (12 g saturated), 58 mg cholesterol, 878 mg sodium, 314 mg potassium.

COTTAGE CHEESE PUFF

This airy baked casserole resembles a soufflé, but without all the fuss.

2 cups cottage cheese
¾ cup soft whole wheat bread crumbs
   (about 1 slice)
½ cup all-purpose flour
⅓ cup snipped parsley
⅓ cup finely chopped green onion
2 tablespoons margarine *or* butter
¼ teaspoon salt
4 eggs
1 tablespoon snipped parsley

In a medium mixing bowl combine cottage cheese, bread crumbs, flour, ⅓ cup parsley, green onion, margarine or butter, and salt. Set aside.

In a large mixing bowl beat eggs with an electric mixer on high speed about 5 minutes or till thick and lemon colored. Gradually pour the cottage cheese mixture over the beaten eggs, folding to combine.

Pour the egg mixture into an ungreased 5- or 6-cup soufflé dish or casserole. Bake in a 350° oven about 1 hour or till a knife inserted near the center comes out clean. Sprinkle with 1 tablespoon parsley. Serve immediately. Makes 6 servings.

Nutrition information per serving: 205 calories, 15 g protein, 12 g carbohydrate, 11 g fat (4 g saturated), 152 mg cholesterol, 490 mg sodium, 147 mg potassium.

VEGETABLE-STUFFED CHAYOTE

Chayote (chaw-YOTE-ee) is a pear-shaped squash with a moist pulp that tastes like a cross between an apple and a cucumber. Look for small, firm, unblemished chayotes and store them in a plastic bag in your refrigerator for up to 2 weeks.

2	medium chayote (8 ounces each)
1	cup sliced fresh mushrooms
½	cup chopped red sweet pepper
1	medium onion, chopped (½ cup)
1	clove garlic, minced
1	tablespoon margarine *or* butter
1½	cups soft whole grain bread crumbs, toasted (2 slices)*
½	cup finely shredded Parmesan cheese
1	beaten egg
2	tablespoons snipped parsley *or* cilantro
⅛	teaspoon salt
⅛	teaspoon pepper
¼	teaspoon instant vegetable *or* chicken bouillon granules
¼	cup water

Halve chayote lengthwise. Place halves in enough cold, salted water to cover. Bring to a boil; reduce heat. Cover and simmer for 12 to 15 minutes or till tender. Drain.

When cool enough to handle, remove seed. Scoop out and reserve pulp to within ¼ inch of skin. Invert shells; set aside to drain. Chop pulp; drain. If necessary, squeeze pulp between paper towels to remove excess liquid. Set aside.

Meanwhile, for stuffing, in a large skillet cook mushrooms, sweet pepper, onion, and garlic in hot margarine or butter till tender but not brown. Remove from heat. Stir in chayote pulp, toasted bread crumbs, ⅓ *cup* of the Parmesan cheese, egg, parsley or cilantro, salt, and pepper. Dissolve the bouillon granules in the water; stir into stuffing. Spoon stuffing into chayote shells.

Place shells in a 2-quart square baking dish. Cover and bake in a 350° oven about 25 minutes or till heated through. Sprinkle with remaining Parmesan cheese. Bake for 3 to 5 minutes more or till cheese melts. Makes 4 servings.

*To toast bread crumbs, spread them in a single layer in a shallow baking pan. Bake in a 350° oven about 8 minutes or till toasted.

Nutrition information per serving: 175 calories, 10 g protein, 16 g carbohydrate, 9 g fat (3 g saturated), 63 mg cholesterol, 428 mg sodium, 401 mg potassium.

CHEESE AND BASIL POLENTA WITH TOMATO-BASIL SAUCE

Polenta (poh-LEN-tuh) is Italian-style cornmeal mush that is made by boiling a mixture of cornmeal and water. This terrific version is layered with two cheeses and basil, baked, and served with a delicate tomato sauce.

2 cups shredded fontina *or* mozzarella
  cheese (8 ounces)
½ cup grated Parmesan *or* Romano
  cheese
2 tablespoons snipped fresh basil
3 cups water
1 cup yellow cornmeal
1 cup cold water
1 teaspoon salt
1 tablespoon margarine *or* butter,
  melted
  Tomato-Basil Sauce
  Fresh basil sprigs (optional)
  Grated Parmesan *or* Romano cheese
  (optional)

In a medium mixing bowl stir together fontina or mozzarella cheese, ½ cup grated Parmesan or Romano cheese, and basil. Set aside.

In a medium saucepan bring 3 cups water to a boil. In a mixing bowl stir together cornmeal, 1 cup cold water, and salt. Slowly add cornmeal mixture to boiling water, stirring constantly. Cook and stir till mixture returns to boiling. Reduce heat to very low. Cover and simmer for 15 minutes, stirring occasionally. Immediately transfer *one-third* of the hot mixture to a greased 2-quart square baking dish. Sprinkle with *half* of the cheese mixture. Repeat layers, ending with the polenta mixture. Cool for 1 hour. Cover with foil and chill several hours or overnight till firm.

To serve, uncover the polenta and bake in a 350° oven about 40 minutes or till lightly browned and heated through. Brush the surface with melted margarine or butter. Let stand for 10 minutes before cutting. Serve with Tomato-Basil Sauce. If desired, garnish with additional basil and sprinkle with Parmesan or Romano cheese. Makes 6 servings.

Tomato-Basil Sauce: In a medium saucepan cook ¾ cup chopped *onion* and 2 cloves *garlic,* minced in 2 tablespoons hot *margarine or butter* till tender but not brown. Carefully stir in two 14½-ounce cans *whole Italian-style tomatoes,* undrained and cut up; half of a 6-ounce can (⅓ cup) *tomato paste;* ½ teaspoon *sugar;* ¼ teaspoon *salt;* and ⅛ teaspoon *pepper.* Bring to a boil; reduce heat. Simmer, uncovered, about 20 minutes or till desired consistency. Stir in ¼ cup snipped *fresh basil.* Cook 5 minutes more. Makes about 3⅓ cups.

Nutrition information per serving: 375 calories, 18 g protein, 31 g carbohydrate, 21 g fat (10 g saturated), 51 mg cholesterol, 1,221 mg sodium, 601 mg potassium.

GINGERED VEGETABLE-TOFU STIR-FRY

Buy extra firm tofu to prevent it from breaking apart while stir-frying this flavorful dish.

1 cup water
¼ cup dry sherry *or* dry white wine
2 tablespoons soy sauce
4 teaspoons cornstarch
½ teaspoon sugar
1 tablespoon cooking oil
2 teaspoons grated gingerroot
1 pound fresh asparagus, cut into
    1-inch pieces (3 cups), *or* one
    10-ounce package frozen cut
    asparagus, thawed and well drained
1 small yellow summer squash, halved
    lengthwise and sliced (1¼ cups)
2 green onions, sliced (¼ cup)
1 10½-ounce package extra firm tofu
    (fresh bean curd), cut into ½-inch
    cubes
½ cup pine nuts *or* chopped almonds,
    toasted
2 cups hot cooked brown rice

For sauce, in a small bowl stir together water, dry sherry or wine, soy sauce, cornstarch, and sugar. Set aside.

Pour the cooking oil into a wok or large skillet. (Add more oil as necessary during cooking.) Preheat the wok or large skillet over medium-high heat. Stir-fry the gingerroot in hot oil for 15 seconds. Add the fresh asparagus (if using) and squash; stir-fry for 3 minutes. Add the thawed asparagus (if using) and green onions; stir-fry about 1½ minutes more or till the asparagus is crisp-tender. Remove vegetables from wok.

Add tofu to the hot wok or skillet. Carefully stir-fry for 2 to 3 minutes or till lightly browned. Remove from wok. Stir the sauce. Add sauce to hot wok. Cook and stir till thickened and bubbly. Return cooked vegetables and tofu to the wok. Stir all ingredients together to coat with sauce. Cover and cook about 1 minute more or till heated through. Stir in pine nuts or almonds. Serve over rice. Makes 4 servings.

Nutrition information per serving: 412 calories, 22 g protein, 38 g carbohydrate, 21 g fat (3 g saturated), 0 mg cholesterol, 541 mg sodium, 576 mg potassium.

MINIATURE MEXICAN FRITTATAS

These spunky little egg casseroles are baked in muffin cups and served with salsa. They make great breakfast or brunch fare.

1   10-ounce package frozen chopped spinach, thawed and well drained
1   cup cottage cheese, drained
½   cup grated Parmesan cheese
½   cup shredded cheddar cheese (2 ounces)
4   eggs
¼   cup milk
1   teaspoon ground cumin
¼   teaspoon pepper
2   tablespoons snipped cilantro *or* parsley
    Salsa, warmed
    Dairy sour cream (optional)

In a medium bowl combine the spinach, cottage cheese, Parmesan cheese, and cheddar cheese. In another bowl stir together the eggs, milk, cumin, and pepper. Stir into spinach mixture. Stir in the cilantro or parsley.

Spoon mixture into 12 lightly greased 2½-inch muffin cups. Bake, uncovered, in a 375° oven for 20 to 25 minutes or till eggs are set. Let stand 5 minutes. Remove from muffin cups. Serve with salsa and, if desired, sour cream. Makes 4 servings.

Nutrition information per serving: 274 calories, 26 g protein, 9 g carbohydrate, 15 g fat (8 g saturated), 244 mg cholesterol, 738 mg sodium, 434 mg potassium.

SAVORY SHEPHERD'S PIE

In a hurry? Substitute packaged instant mashed potatoes (enough for 4 servings) for the 3 medium potatoes and stir the garlic mixture into the prepared instant potatoes.

3 small potatoes (¾ pound)
2 cloves garlic, minced
½ teaspoon dried basil, crushed
2 tablespoons margarine *or* butter
¼ teaspoon salt
2 to 4 tablespoons milk
1 medium onion, chopped (½ cup)
1 medium carrot, sliced (½ cup)
1 tablespoon cooking oil
1 15-ounce can kidney beans, rinsed
    and drained
1 14½-ounce can whole tomatoes,
    drained and cut up
1 10-ounce package frozen whole
    kernel corn *or* mixed vegetables
1 8-ounce can tomato sauce
1 teaspoon Worcestershire sauce
½ teaspoon sugar
1 cup shredded cheddar cheese
    (4 ounces)
   Paprika (optional)

Peel and quarter potatoes. Cook, covered, in a small amount of boiling lightly salted water for 20 to 25 minutes or till tender. Drain. Mash with a potato masher or beat with an electric mixer on low speed. In a small saucepan cook garlic and dried basil in margarine or butter for 15 seconds. Add to mashed potatoes along with salt. Gradually beat in enough milk to make light and fluffy. Set aside.

For filling, in a medium saucepan cook onion and carrot in hot oil till onion is tender but not brown. Stir in kidney beans, tomatoes, frozen vegetables, tomato sauce, Worcestershire sauce, and sugar. Heat till bubbly.

Transfer vegetable mixture to an 8x8x2-inch square baking pan. Drop mashed potatoes in 4 mounds over vegetable mixture. Sprinkle with cheddar cheese and, if desired, paprika. Bake, uncovered, in a 375° oven for 25 to 30 minutes or till heated through and cheese begins to brown. Makes 4 servings.

Nutrition information per serving: 456 calories, 20 g protein, 60 g carbohydrate, 19 g fat (8 g saturated), 31 mg cholesterol, 1,130 mg sodium, 1,091 mg potassium.

WHEAT BERRY-WATERCRESS QUICHE

Watercress gives this quiche a peppery bite while wheat berries and egg whites give it a healthy face-lift. If you have trouble finding wheat berries at your local health food store, substitute ⅔ cup cooked wild rice.

1   9-inch unbaked pastry shell
2   eggs
2   egg whites
1½ cups milk
1   tablespoon Dijon-style mustard
½   cup coarsely chopped watercress
      leaves
¼   cup sliced green onion
¼   teaspoon salt
¼   teaspoon pepper
⅔   cup cooked wheat berries*
1½ cups shredded Swiss cheese
      (6 ounces)

Line the bottom of pastry shell with a double thickness of foil. Bake in a 450° oven for 8 minutes. Remove foil; bake 4 to 5 minutes more or till set and dry. Set aside. Reduce oven temperature to 325°. In a bowl stir together eggs, egg whites, milk, mustard, watercress leaves, green onion, salt, and pepper.

Sprinkle cooked wheat berries in the bottom of pastry shell. Top with shredded Swiss cheese. Slowly pour egg mixture over wheat berry mixture. Bake in a 325° oven about 50 minutes or till a knife inserted near the center comes out clean. If necessary, cover edge of crust with foil to prevent overbrowning. Let stand for 10 minutes. Makes 6 servings.

*To cook wheat berries, in a small saucepan bring 1 cup *water* and ⅓ cup *uncooked wheat berries* to a boil; reduce heat. Cover and simmer for 1 hour. Drain well on paper towels.

Nutrition information per serving: 433 calories, 19 g protein, 39 g carbohydrate, 23 g fat (9 g saturated), 101 mg cholesterol, 387 mg sodium, 298 mg potassium.

WARM BEANS WITH HERBED TOMATOES AND GOAT CHEESE

Get extra mileage out of this recipe by chilling any leftovers and serve them as salad with warm tortillas.

3   medium ripe tomatoes, seeded and chopped (1½ cups)
¼   cup snipped fresh basil
¼   cup snipped fresh oregano
2   green onions, sliced (¼ cup)
1   clove garlic, minced
½   teaspoon salt
¼   teaspoon pepper
1   15-ounce can small red beans *or* kidney beans
1   15-ounce can great northern beans *or* navy beans
4   ounces semi-soft goat cheese *or* feta cheese, crumbled (1 cup)
     Fresh basil sprigs (optional)

In a medium bowl combine tomatoes, fresh basil, fresh oregano, green onions, garlic, salt, and pepper. Let stand at room temperature for 30 minutes to 2 hours.

In a medium saucepan combine *undrained* red or kidney beans and *undrained* great northern or navy beans. Bring to a boil; reduce heat. Cover and simmer for 2 minutes or till heated through. Drain.

To serve, toss warm beans with tomato mixture. Sprinkle cheese over bean mixture. If desired, garnish with fresh basil. Serve warm. Makes 4 servings.

Nutrition information per serving: 304 calories, 22 g protein, 45 g carbohydrate, 7 g fat (4 g saturated), 13 mg cholesterol, 558 mg sodium, 796 mg potassium.

TWO-BEAN TAMALE PIE

This mildly-seasoned kidney and pinto bean casserole is topped with a crusty cornbread hat. Garnish it with sliced fresh chili peppers and snipped cilantro, then serve it to your family along with your favorite salsa.

1 medium green pepper, chopped
   (¾ cup)
1 small onion, chopped (⅓ cup)
2 cloves garlic, minced
1 tablespoon cooking oil
1 15-ounce can kidney beans, rinsed,
   drained, and slightly mashed
1 15-ounce can pinto beans, rinsed,
   drained, and slightly mashed
1 6-ounce can (⅔ cup) vegetable juice
   cocktail
¼ cup snipped cilantro *or* parsley
1 teaspoon chili powder
1 teaspoon ground cumin
½ cup yellow cornmeal
½ cup whole wheat flour
1 teaspoon baking soda
¼ teaspoon salt
1 egg
½ cup buttermilk
1 4-ounce can chopped green chili
   peppers
2 tablespoons cooking oil
½ cup shredded cheddar cheese
   (2 ounces)

Grease a 10-inch quiche dish or a 2-quart square baking dish; set aside. In a medium skillet cook green pepper, onion, and garlic in 1 tablespoon hot oil till tender but not brown. Stir in the kidney beans, pinto beans, vegetable juice cocktail, cilantro or parsley, chili powder, and cumin. Heat through. Spoon the bean mixture into prepared baking dish.

In a medium bowl stir together the cornmeal, flour, baking soda, and salt. Combine egg, buttermilk, green chili peppers, and 2 tablespoons oil. Add to cornmeal mixture, stirring just till combined. Fold in cheese. Spread cornmeal mixture evenly over the top of the bean mixture. Bake, uncovered, in a 400° oven about 20 minutes or till golden brown. Makes 6 servings.

Nutrition information per serving: 330 calories, 16 g protein, 45 g carbohydrate, 12 g fat (3 g saturated), 46 mg cholesterol, 856 mg sodium, 477 mg potassium.

SPINACH-RICE CASSEROLE

You can make 4 individual casseroles or 1 large casserole with this recipe. Be sure to thaw the spinach before you start.

1   small onion, chopped (⅓ cup)
1   clove garlic, minced
1   tablespoon cooking oil
1   14½-ounce can peeled Italian-style
     tomatoes, cut up
1   teaspoon dried oregano *or* basil,
     crushed
8   ounces tofu (fresh bean curd), drained
2   cups cooked brown rice
1   10-ounce package frozen chopped
     spinach, thawed and well drained
½   cup shredded Swiss cheese (2 ounces)
½   teaspoon salt
¼   teaspoon pepper
1   tablespoon sesame seed, toasted

In a large saucepan cook the onion and garlic in hot oil till onion is tender but not brown. Add *undrained* tomatoes and oregano or basil. Bring to a boil; reduce heat. Simmer, uncovered, about 3 minutes.

Meanwhile, place tofu in a food processor bowl or blender container. Cover and process or blend till smooth. Add to tomato mixture. Stir in cooked rice, spinach, *half* of the Swiss cheese, salt, and pepper.

Grease 4 individual casseroles or one 2-quart rectangular baking dish. Spoon mixture into casseroles. Bake, uncovered, in a 350° oven for 30 to 40 minutes or till heated through. Sprinkle with remaining cheese and sesame seed. Makes 4 servings.

Nutrition information per serving: 301 calories, 15 g protein, 36 g carbohydrate, 12 g fat (4 g saturated), 13 mg cholesterol, 701 mg sodium, 647 mg potassium.

COUSCOUS TACOS

Couscous (KOOS-koos) is a quick-cooking grain made from ground semolina in the shape of very tiny beads. Look for it in the rice or pasta section of your supermarket or at specialty stores.

1 14½-ounce can Mexican-style stewed
    tomatoes
1 cup water
¼ cup chopped onion
½ of a 1⅛- or 1¼-ounce envelope
    (5 teaspoons) taco seasoning mix
⅔ cup couscous
8 ounces firm *or* extra-firm tofu
    (fresh bean curd), drained and
    finely chopped
10 taco shells, warmed
1½ cups shredded lettuce
⅔ cup shredded cheddar cheese
    (about 3 ounces)
    Salsa

In a medium saucepan combine *undrained* stewed tomatoes, water, onion, and taco seasoning mix. Bring to a boil. Stir in couscous and tofu. Cover; remove from heat. Let stand for 5 minutes.

Spoon couscous mixture into taco shells. Top with lettuce and cheese. Serve with salsa. Makes 5 servings.

Nutrition information per serving: 365 calories, 18 g protein, 45 g carbohydrate, 15 g fat (4 g saturated), 16 mg cholesterol, 809 mg sodium, 475 mg potassium.

SPAGHETTI SQUASH ITALIANO

Save time by cooking spaghetti squash in your microwave oven. Prick whole squash with a sharp knife. Place squash in a microwave-safe baking dish. Micro-cook, uncovered, on 100% power (high) for 15 to 20 minutes or till tender. Let stand 5 minutes. Halve squash lengthwise and remove seeds.

2   small spaghetti squash (1¼ to 1½ pounds)
4   ounces mozzarella cheese, cut into small cubes (1 cup)
3   medium tomatoes, seeded and chopped (1½ cups)
4   green onions, sliced (½ cup)
½   cup pine nuts *or* coarsely chopped walnuts, toasted
¼   cup snipped fresh basil *or* parsley
1   tablespoon olive oil *or* cooking oil
2   cloves garlic, minced
2   tablespoons grated Parmesan cheese

Halve squash lengthwise and remove the seeds. Prick skin all over. Place halves, cut side down, in a 3-quart rectangular baking dish. Cover and bake in a 350° oven for 60 to 70 minutes or till tender. Using a fork, separate the squash pulp into strands, leaving strands in shell. Sprinkle *one-fourth* of the mozzarella cheese in *each* shell; toss lightly. Press mixture up the sides of the shell.

Meanwhile, in a bowl combine tomatoes, green onions, nuts, basil or parsley, oil, and garlic. Spoon *one-fourth* of the tomato mixture into *each* shell. Sprinkle with Parmesan cheese. Return to baking dish. Return to oven and bake, uncovered, about 20 minutes or till filling is heated through. Makes 4 servings.

Nutrition information per serving: 304 calories, 15 g protein, 23 g carbohydrate, 20 g fat (6 g saturated), 18 mg cholesterol, 237 mg sodium, 665mg potassium.

VEGETARIAN LENTIL PAELLA

Traditional Spanish paella contains chicken, seafood, rice, and vegetables. This hearty meatless version uses lentils and a colorful medley of vegetables and seasonings.

1 medium green pepper, chopped
  (1 cup)
1 medium yellow sweet pepper,
  chopped (1 cup)
2 stalks celery, sliced (1 cup)
1 medium onion, chopped (½ cup)
1 medium red onion, chopped (½ cup)
4 cloves garlic, minced
2 tablespoons olive oil *or* cooking oil
1 cup lentils
1¾ cups vegetable *or* chicken broth
⅛ teaspoon powdered saffron *or*
  ½ teaspoon ground turmeric
2 medium tomatoes, seeded and
  chopped (1 cup)
1 cup frozen peas, thawed
⅓ cup pimiento-stuffed olives
⅓ cup pitted ripe olives
¼ cup snipped cilantro *or* parsley

In a Dutch oven cook the green pepper, yellow pepper, celery, onion, red onion, and garlic in hot oil till onion is tender but not brown. Rinse lentils. Add lentils, vegetable or chicken broth, and saffron or turmeric to the pepper mixture. Bring to a boil; reduce heat. Cover and simmer for 20 to 30 minutes or till lentils are tender and liquid is absorbed. Stir in tomatoes, peas, stuffed olives, ripe olives, and cilantro or parsley. Heat through. Season to taste before serving. Makes 4 servings.

Nutrition information per serving: 306 calories, 16 g protein, 46 g carbohydrate, 10 g fat (1g saturated), 0 mg cholesterol, 1,034 mg sodium, 913 mg potassium.

CHILLED CHEESE AND NUT LOAF

Serve this delightfully different entree with a fresh green salad and crunchy whole grain bread sticks. Or, transform it into an appetizer and take it to your next party.

1   medium onion, chopped (½ cup)
2   cloves garlic, minced
1   tablespoon margarine *or* butter
1½   cups shredded sharp cheddar cheese
       (6 ounces)
1   8-ounce package cream cheese, cut up
       and softened
2   cups cream-style cottage cheese
¾   cup finely ground almonds *or* pine
       nuts
½   cup milk
2   tablespoons Dijon-style mustard
1   teaspoon ground cumin
½   teaspoon pepper
¼   cup snipped cilantro *or* parsley
1   2-ounce jar chopped pimientos,
       drained
     Lettuce leaves
1   8-ounce container soft-style cream
       cheese
     Assorted sliced vegetables,
       condiments, *and/or* fresh herbs
       (such as radishes, red and yellow
       sweet peppers, olives, pine nuts,
       or cilantro)
     Salsa

In a small skillet cook onion and garlic in hot margarine or butter till tender but not brown. In a large mixing bowl combine onion mixture, cheddar cheese, 8 ounces cream cheese, cottage cheese, nuts, milk, mustard, cumin, and pepper. Beat with an electric mixer on medium speed till nearly smooth. (Or, for a smoother consistency, process half of the mixture at a time in a food processor.) Stir in the cilantro or parsley and pimientos.

Spread cheese mixture evenly into a greased and foil-lined 9x5x3-inch loaf pan. Bake in a 325° oven about 1 hour or till top is golden (mixture will not be set). Cool completely in pan on a wire rack. Cover and chill for 4 to 24 hours.

To serve, loosen sides of loaf with a table knife. Invert onto a lettuce-lined serving platter. Spread 8 ounces soft-style cream cheese over the top of loaf. Garnish with vegetables, condiments, and/or herbs. Serve with salsa. Makes 8 servings.

Nutrition information per serving: 437 calories, 21 g protein, 10 g carbohydrate, 36 g fat (18 g saturated), 90 mg cholesterol, 664 mg sodium, 291 mg potassium.

SOUTH-OF-THE-BORDER PIE

Beans, rice, eggs, and cheese provide the protein while chili powder and cumin provide the kick. Serve this with a simple tossed salad.

1   medium onion, chopped (½ cup)
2   cloves garlic, minced
1   tablespoon olive oil *or* cooking oil
1   to 2 teaspoons chili powder
1   teaspoon ground cumin
¼   teaspoon salt
1   15-ounce can red kidney beans,
     rinsed and drained
1½ cups cooked brown rice
1   cup shredded cheddar cheese
     (4 ounces)
¾   cup milk
2   beaten eggs
     Nonstick spray coating
     Chopped green pepper (optional)
     Salsa (optional)

In a saucepan cook onion and garlic in hot oil till tender but not brown. Stir in chili powder, cumin, and salt. Cook for 1 minute more. Cool. Stir in beans, cooked rice, cheese, milk, and eggs.

Spray a 10-inch pie plate or quiche dish with nonstick coating. Spoon mixture into pie plate. Bake, uncovered, in a 350° degree oven about 25 minutes or till the center is set. Let stand 10 minutes. If desired, sprinkle with green pepper and serve with salsa. Makes 6 servings.

Nutrition information per serving: 254 calories, 14 g protein, 26 g carbohydrate, 12 g fat (5 g saturated), 93 mg cholesterol, 366 mg sodium, 260 mg potassium.

SOUTHERN GRITS CASSEROLE WITH RED PEPPER RELISH

To make a roasted pepper relish, halve 3 medium peppers and place them, cut side down, on a foil-lined baking sheet. Bake in a 425° oven for 20 to 25 minutes or till skin is bubbly and browned. Place in a new paper bag; seal and let stand for 30 minutes or till cool enough to handle. Peel skin. Chop and stir into cooked onion mixture.

4   cups water
1   cup quick-cooking grits
4   beaten eggs
2   cups shredded cheddar cheese
       (8 ounces)
½   cup milk
2   green onions, sliced (¼ cup)
1   to 2 jalapeño peppers, seeded
       (if desired) and chopped
½   teaspoon garlic salt
¼   teaspoon white pepper
     Sliced green onion (optional)
2   medium red sweet peppers, chopped
       (2 cups)
1   small red onion, chopped (½ cup)
2   cloves garlic, minced
1   tablespoon margarine *or* butter
⅓   cup snipped parsley
1   tablespoon white wine vinegar

In a large saucepan bring water to a boil. Slowly stir in grits. Gradually stir about *1 cup* of the hot mixture into the eggs. Return to saucepan. Remove from heat. Stir in cheese, milk, green onion, jalepeño peppers, garlic salt, and white pepper.

Spoon grits mixture into a 2-quart casserole. Bake, uncovered, in a 350° oven for 45 to 50 minutes or till a knife inserted near the center comes out clean. If desired, sprinkle with additional green onion.

Meanwhile, for relish, in a medium saucepan cook red peppers, red onion, and garlic in hot margarine or butter till peppers are just tender. Remove from heat and stir in parsley and vinegar. Let stand at room temperature at least 30 minutes. Serve with grits. Makes 4 servings.

Nutrition information per serving: 403 calories, 23 g protein, 16 g carbohydrate, 27 g fat (14 g saturated), 275 mg cholesterol, 731 mg sodium, 321 mg potassium.

ITALIAN ARTICHOKE PIE

Not only does this make a super supper dish, it's also great for a late-morning brunch.

3   beaten eggs
1   3-ounce package cream cheese with
      chives, softened
¾   teaspoon garlic powder
¼   teaspoon pepper
1½   cups shredded mozzarella cheese
      (6 ounces)
1   cup ricotta cheese
½   cup mayonnaise *or* salad dressing
1   14-ounce can artichoke hearts,
      drained
½   of a 15-ounce can (¾ cup) garbanzo
      beans, rinsed and drained
1   2¼-ounce can sliced pitted ripe
      olives, drained
1   2-ounce jar diced pimientos, drained
2   tablespoons snipped parsley
1   unbaked 9-inch pastry shell
⅓   cup grated Parmesan cheese
2   small tomatoes, sliced

In a large mixing bowl stir together eggs, cream cheese, garlic powder, and pepper. Add *1 cup* of the mozzarella cheese, ricotta cheese, and mayonnaise or salad dressing. Stir till thoroughly combined.

Quarter *2* artichoke hearts; set aside. Chop remaining hearts. Fold chopped hearts, garbanzo beans, olives, pimientos, and parsley into the cheese mixture. Pour into pastry shell.

Bake in a 350° oven for 30 minutes. Top with the remaining mozzarella cheese and Parmesan cheese. Bake about 15 minutes more or till set. Let stand for 10 minutes. Arrange tomato slices and quartered artichoke hearts over the top. Cut into wedges. Makes 8 servings.

Nutrition information per serving: 764 calories, 36 g protein, 51 g carbohydrate, 47 g fat (20 g saturated), 234 mg cholesterol, 1,152 mg sodium, 618 mg potassium.

SPICY BLACK BEANS AND RICE

Instead of rice, spoon the warm black bean mixture over squares of freshly baked corn bread.

1 medium onion, chopped (½ cup)
4 cloves garlic, minced
2 tablespoons olive oil *or* cooking oil
1 15-ounce can black beans, rinsed and drained
1 14½-ounce can Mexican-style stewed tomatoes
⅛ to ¼ teaspoon ground red pepper
2 cups hot cooked brown *or* long grain rice
¼ cup chopped onion (optional)

In a medium saucepan cook ½ cup onion and garlic in hot oil till tender but not brown. Carefully stir in the drained beans, *undrained* tomatoes, and ground red pepper. Bring to a boil; reduce heat. Simmer, uncovered, for 15 minutes.

To serve, mound rice on individual plates; make a well in the centers. Spoon black bean mixture into centers. If desired, sprinkle with chopped onion. Makes 4 servings.

Nutrition information per serving: 279 calories, 11 g protein, 47 g carbohydrate, 8 g fat (1 g saturated), 0 mg cholesterol, 631 mg sodium, 573 mg potassium.

CRISPY EGGPLANT WITH SPICY TOMATO-FETA CHEESE SAUCE

For a mild cheese flavor, sprinkle feta cheese over the spaghetti sauce. For a more robust cheese flavor, use blue cheese.

1   medium eggplant (about 1 pound), peeled and thinly sliced
     Salt
2   eggs
2   tablespoons milk
½   cup grated Parmesan cheese
½   cup toasted wheat germ
1   teaspoon dried basil, crushed
¼   teaspoon pepper
2   cups meatless spaghetti sauce
¼   to ½ teaspoon ground red pepper
1   cup crumbled feta *or* blue cheese
     Fresh snipped basil *or* parsley (optional)

Place eggplant slices on a baking sheet. Lightly salt eggplant. Let stand for 10 minutes. Pat dry with paper towels.

In a shallow bowl combine the eggs and milk. In another shallow bowl stir together the Parmesan cheese, wheat germ, basil, and pepper. Dip the eggplant slices in egg mixture, then into wheat germ mixture, turning to coat both sides. Place the coated slices in a single layer on a greased baking sheet. Bake, uncovered, in a 400° oven for 15 to 20 minutes or till the eggplant is crisp on the outside and tender on the inside.

Meanwhile, for sauce, in a medium saucepan combine the spaghetti sauce and ground red pepper. Cook over medium heat till heated through.

To serve, place several slices of eggplant on individual plates. Spoon tomato sauce over eggplant. Sprinkle with feta or blue cheese and, if desired, fresh basil or parsley. Makes 4 servings.

Nutrition information per serving: 388 calories, 20 g protein, 35 g carbohydrate, 20 g fat (9 g saturated), 142 mg cholesterol, 1,471 mg sodium, 906 mg potassium.

GOLDEN FETTUCCINE SOUFFLÉ

Baby food carrots help make this soufflé golden and save you time in the kitchen. But if you prefer to use fresh carrots, cook 2 cups chopped or sliced carrots in a small amount of lightly salted boiling water for 20 minutes or till tender. Drain well. Purée in a food processor or blender.

4 ounces fettuccine *or* linguine, broken into 1-inch pieces (1⅓ cups)
¼ cup chopped onion
1 clove garlic, minced
3 tablespoons margarine *or* butter
¼ cup all-purpose flour
2 teaspoons snipped fresh dill *or* ½ teaspoon dried dillweed
½ teaspoon salt
¼ teaspoon pepper
1 cup milk
3 4-ounce jars puréed baby food carrots
2 egg yolks
4 egg whites

Cook fettuccine according to package directions. Drain. Meanwhile, in a medium saucepan cook onion and garlic in hot margarine or butter till tender but not brown. Stir in flour, fresh dill or dillweed, salt, and pepper. Add milk all at once. Cook and stir till thickened and bubbly. Remove from heat. Stir in baby food carrots and cooked fettuccine. In a medium bowl, beat egg yolks with a fork till combined. Gradually add carrot mixture, stirring constantly. Set aside.

In a large bowl beat egg whites till stiff peaks form (tips stand straight). Gently fold about *1 cup* of the beaten egg whites into the carrot mixture. Gradually pour carrot mixture over remaining egg whites, folding to combine. Pour into an ungreased 1½-quart soufflé dish or a 2-quart square baking dish.

Bake, uncovered, in a 350° oven for 35 to 40 minutes or till a knife inserted near the center comes out clean. Serve immediately. Makes 4 servings.

Nutrition information per serving: 310 calories, 12 g protein, 36 g carbohydrate, 13 g fat (3 g saturated), 111 mg cholesterol, 480 mg sodium, 321 mg potassium.

TOFU SKILLET LASAGNA

Instead of lasagna noodles, you assemble this one-dish meal with thinly sliced tofu and cook it on the stove top in a large skillet.

1   15½-ounce jar meatless spaghetti
      sauce with mushrooms (1½ cups)
1   8- or 10½-ounce package firm tofu
      (fresh bean curd), drained
3   cups loose-pack frozen broccoli,
      French-style green beans, onions,
      and red peppers
1   cup ricotta cheese
¼   cup grated Parmesan cheese
½   teaspoon dried oregano, crushed
¼   teaspoon pepper
½   cup shredded cheddar *or* mozzarella
      cheese (2 ounces)

In a large skillet heat *1¼ cups* of the spaghetti sauce over low heat. Thinly slice the tofu and arrange *half* of the slices in the skillet with sauce. Run cool water over the vegetables in a colander to thaw. Squeeze with hands to remove excess liquid. Sprinkle vegetables into skillet.

Stir together the ricotta cheese, Parmesan cheese, oregano, and pepper. Drop by spoonfuls over vegetable mixture. Top with remaining tofu slices and spaghetti sauce. Cover and cook over low heat for 10 to 15 minutes or till mixture is heated through. Sprinkle with cheddar or mozzarella cheese before serving. Makes 4 servings.

Nutrition information per serving: 369 calories, 26 g protein, 27 g carbohydrate, 19 g fat (7 g saturated), 32 mg cholesterol, 827 mg sodium, 765 mg potassium.

LAYERED POTATOES AND LEEKS

This easy-on-the-cook casserole is layered with a savory leek and mushroom mixture, sliced potatoes, and Parmesan cheese. Serve it with a simple salad of mixed greens and vinaigrette dressing.

2   medium leeks, thinly sliced (⅔ cup)
8   ounces fresh mushrooms, sliced
      (3 cups)
2   cloves garlic, minced
½   teaspoon dried rosemary, crushed
1   tablespoon olive oil *or* cooking oil
3   cups ¼-inch thick sliced unpeeled
      potatoes (about 1 pound)
¾   cup grated Parmesan cheese
1   tablespoon olive oil *or* cooking oil
1   8-ounce carton plain yogurt *or* dairy
      sour cream

In a large skillet cook the leeks, mushrooms, garlic, and rosemary in 1 tablespoon hot oil till leeks are tender but not brown. Meanwhile, bring a large pot of lightly salted water to a boil; add potatoes. Return to boiling; reduce heat. Cover and simmer for 3 minutes. Drain. (Potatoes will not be tender.)

Grease a 1½-quart soufflé dish or casserole. Arrange *1 cup* of the potato slices over the bottom of the dish, overlapping slices if necessary. Spoon *one-third* of the leek mixture (about ⅔ cup) over potatoes. Sprinkle with *¼ cup* of the Parmesan cheese. Repeat layering twice. Drizzle top layer with 1 tablespoon oil. Bake, uncovered, in a 400° oven for 35 to 40 minutes or till potatoes are golden brown and tender. Let stand 10 minutes. Serve with yogurt or sour cream. Makes 4 servings.

Nutrition information per serving: 319 calories, 15 g protein, 36 g carbohydrate, 14 g fat (5 g saturated), 18 mg cholesterol, 402 mg sodium, 843 mg potassium.

CHEESE TORTELLINI WITH CANELLINI BEAN SAUCE

You can make this low-fat pasta dish in a snap thanks to refrigerated tortellini and canned beans. Try it for a busy week night dinner.

1   9-ounce package refrigerated cheese-stuffed tortellini
1   15-ounce can canellini beans, rinsed and drained
⅔   cup milk
¼   cup grated Parmesan cheese
⅓   cup thin slivers of red *and/or* yellow sweet pepper
⅓   cup thin slivers of green pepper
1   tablespoon chopped fresh oregano *or* 1 teaspoon dried oregano, crushed
¼   teaspoon salt
¼   teaspoon ground nutmeg
⅛   teaspoon freshly ground pepper
     Shredded Parmesan cheese (optional)
     Fresh oregano sprigs (optional)

Cook tortellini according to package directions. Drain. Meanwhile, place the beans and milk in a food processor bowl or blender container. Cover and process or blend till smooth. Transfer to a large skillet. Stir in grated Parmesan cheese, red and/or yellow pepper, green pepper, oregano, salt, nutmeg, and pepper. Cook and stir till heated through. Serve sauce over drained tortellini. If desired, sprinkle with shredded Parmesan cheese and garnish with fresh oregano. Makes 4 servings.

Nutrition information per serving: 304 calories, 21 g protein, 48 g carbohydrate, 6 g fat (2 g saturated), 43 mg cholesterol, 730 mg sodium, 272 mg potassium.

FRESH VEGETABLE RISOTTO

Classic risotto is an Italian short grain rice simmered and constantly stirred so it slowly absorbs the cooking liquid, resulting in a creamy, delicious dish. This one is flavored with colorful vegetables and two cheeses.

2 cups sliced fresh mushrooms
1 medium onion, chopped (½ cup)
2 cloves garlic, minced
2 tablespoons olive oil *or* cooking oil
1 cup Arborio *or* long grain rice
3 cups vegetable *or* chicken broth
¾ cup bite-size asparagus *or* broccoli pieces
1 medium tomato, seeded and diced (¾ cup)
¼ cup shredded carrot
1 cup shredded fontina *or* Muenster cheese (4 ounces)
¼ cup grated Parmesan cheese
3 tablespoons snipped fresh basil *or* parsley
   Tomato slices (optional)

In a large saucepan cook the mushrooms, onion, and garlic in hot oil till onion is tender but not brown. Stir in the rice. Cook and stir for 5 minutes.

Meanwhile, in another saucepan bring the vegetable or chicken broth to a boil; reduce heat and simmer. Slowly add *1 cup* of the broth to the rice mixture, stirring constantly. Continue to cook and stir till liquid is absorbed. Add *½ cup* broth and the asparagus or broccoli to the rice mixture, stirring constantly. Continue to cook and stir till liquid is absorbed. Add *1 cup* more broth, *½ cup* at a time, stirring constantly till the broth has been absorbed. This should take about 15 minutes. Stir in tomato, carrot, and the remaining ½ cup broth. Cook and stir till rice is slightly creamy and just tender. Stir in fontina or Muenster cheese, Parmesan cheese, and basil or parsley. If desired, garnish with some tomato slices. Serve immediately. Makes 4 servings.

Nutrition information per serving: 401 calories, 15 g protein, 47 g carbohydrate, 19 g fat (8 g saturated), 38 mg cholesterol, 1,052 mg sodium, 386 mg potassium.

FOUR BEAN ENCHILADAS

Using canned beans makes this dish a snap to prepare. We chose kidney, garbanzo, pinto, and navy beans but you can use any combination of beans that you like.

16 6-inch corn tortillas
 1 15-ounce can red kidney beans,
    rinsed and drained
 1 15-ounce can garbanzo beans, rinsed
    and drained
 1 15-ounce can pinto beans, rinsed and
    drained
 1 15-ounce can navy *or* great northern
    beans, rinsed and drained
 1 11-ounce can condensed cheddar
    cheese *or* nacho cheese soup
 1 10-ounce can enchilada sauce
 1 8-ounce can tomato sauce
1½ cups shredded Monterey Jack *or*
    cheddar cheese (6 ounces)
    Sliced pitted ripe olives (optional)
    Chopped green pepper (optional)

Stack tortillas and wrap tightly in foil. Bake in a 350° oven for 10 minutes or till warm.

For filling, combine beans and cheese soup. Spoon about ⅓ *cup* filling onto one end of *each* tortilla. Starting at the end with the filling, roll up each tortilla. Arrange tortillas, seam side down, in 8 individual au gratin dishes or two 2-quart rectangular baking dishes.

In a bowl stir together the enchilada sauce and tomato sauce; pour over tortillas. Cover with foil. Bake in a 350° oven for 20 minutes for au gratin dishes or 30 minutes for baking dishes or till heated through. Remove foil; sprinkle with cheese. Bake, uncovered, about 5 minutes more or till cheese melts. If desired, sprinkle with olives and green pepper. Makes 8 servings.

Nutrition information per serving: 491 calories, 25 g protein, 71 g carbohydrate, 14 g fat (7 g saturated), 29 mg cholesterol, 1,599 mg sodium, 718 mg potassium.

PASTA-BEAN SOUP WITH FRESH HERBS

Fresh basil and thyme take all the credit for the terrific taste of this soup. Do yourself a favor and use only fresh herbs.

2   cups sliced fresh mushrooms
1   medium onion, chopped (½ cup)
2   cloves garlic, minced
1   tablespoon margarine *or* butter
2   14½-ounce cans vegetable, chicken,
      or beef broth
½   cup small pasta shells
1   16-ounce can tomatoes, cut up
1   15-ounce can garbanzo beans, rinsed
      and drained
¼   cup snipped fresh basil
1   tablespoon snipped fresh thyme
      Fresh basil sprigs (optional)

In a large saucepan or Dutch oven cook the mushrooms, onion, and garlic in hot margarine or butter till tender but not brown. Add vegetable, chicken, or beef broth. Bring to a boil. Stir in the pasta. Return to a boil. Cook for 10 to 12 minutes or till pasta is al dente (tender but still firm). Stir in *undrained* tomatoes and garbanzo beans. Heat through.

Just before serving, stir in fresh basil and thyme. To serve, ladle soup into individual bowls. If desired, garnish with fresh basil. Makes 4 servings.

Nutrition information per serving: 213 calories, 9 g protein, 38 g carbohydrate, 6 g fat (1 g saturated), 0 mg cholesterol, 1,494 mg sodium, 658 mg potassium.

POTATO-PINTO BEAN SOUP

Fragrant fresh basil flavors this hearty bean soup. If you can't find fresh, use ½ teaspoon dried basil and stir it in when you add the broth.

1 medium onion, chopped (½ cup)
1 cup sliced shiitake *or* button
      mushrooms
2 teaspoons olive oil *or* cooking oil
3 large potatoes, peeled and thinly
      sliced (4 ½ cups)
2 14½-ounce cans vegetable, chicken,
      or beef broth
1 15-ounce can pinto beans, rinsed and
      drained
½ cup buttermilk
1 tablespoon cornstarch
1 tablespoon snipped fresh basil
¼ cup plain yogurt *or* dairy sour cream
    Fresh basil sprigs (optional)

In a large saucepan cook the onion and mushrooms in hot oil till onion is tender but not brown. Add the potatoes and broth. Bring to a boil; reduce heat. Cover and simmer about 30 minutes or till potatoes are tender. Stir in beans.

In a small bowl stir together the buttermilk and cornstarch; stir into potato mixture. Cook and stir till thickened and bubbly. Cook and stir for 2 minutes more. Stir in 1 tablespoon snipped basil.

To serve, ladle soup into individual bowls. Dollop each serving with yogurt or sour cream. If desired, garnish with fresh basil. Makes 4 servings.

Nutrition information per serving: 273 calories, 11 g protein, 56 g carbohydrate, 4 g fat (1 g saturated), 2 mg cholesterol, 1,231 mg sodium, 725 mg potassium.

CORN AND GREEN CHILI CHOWDER

During sweet corn season, you can make this chowder using fresh ears of corn. Omit the frozen corn and use a sharp knife to remove the kernels from 2 medium ears of sweet corn.

1   medium onion, chopped (½ cup)
2   tablespoons margarine *or* butter
2   tablespoons all-purpose flour
2   cups water
1   large potato, peeled and diced (1 cup)
1   10-ounce package frozen whole
       kernel corn
1   4-ounce can chopped green chili
       peppers
1   tablespoon instant vegetable *or*
       chicken bouillon granules
¼   teaspoon coarsely ground pepper
2   cups milk
2   tablespoons snipped cilantro *or*
       parsley
     Cilantro *or* parsley sprigs (optional)
     Sliced fresh chili peppers (optional)

In a large saucepan cook onion in hot margarine or butter till tender but not brown. Stir in flour. Add water, potato, frozen corn, chili peppers, bouillon granules, and pepper. Bring to a boil; reduce heat. Cover and simmer about 10 minutes or till potatoes are tender. Stir in the milk and 2 tablespoons cilantro or parsley; heat through.

To serve, ladle chowder into individual bowls. If desired, garnish each serving with additional cilantro or parsley sprigs and sliced fresh chili peppers. Makes 4 servings.

Nutrition information per serving: 234 calories, 8 g protein, 34 g carbohydrate, 9 g fat (1 g saturated), 9 mg cholesterol, 944 mg sodium, 486 mg potassium.

LIMA BEAN GAZPACHO

At taste panel, even our lima bean hater loved this soup! Serve it with crusty bread for a real warm weather treat.

1 10-ounce package baby lima beans
3 medium tomatoes, peeled and
     coarsely chopped (about 2 cups)
1 small green pepper, chopped (½ cup)
1 small yellow sweet pepper, chopped
     (½ cup)
1 small cucumber, chopped (1 cup)
2 green onions, sliced (¼ cup)
1 clove garlic, minced
1 11½-ounce can (1½ cups) vegetable
     juice cocktail
3 tablespoons balsamic *or* red wine
     vinegar
1 tablespoon chopped fresh dill *or*
     1 teaspoon dried dillweed
¼ teaspoon salt
   Several dashes bottled hot pepper
     sauce
⅓ cup plain yogurt *or* dairy sour cream
   Finely shredded lime peel

Cook lima beans according to package directions; drain. In a large mixing bowl combine cooked lima beans, tomatoes, green pepper, yellow pepper, cucumber, onions, and garlic. Stir in vegetable juice cocktail, vinegar, dill or dillweed, salt, and hot pepper sauce. Cover and chill for several hours.

To serve, ladle soup into individual bowls. Dollop each serving with yogurt or sour cream and garnish with shredded lime peel. Makes 4 servings.

Nutrition information per serving: 150 calories, 7 g protein, 29 g carbohydrate, 1 g fat (0 g saturated), 1 mg cholesterol, 493 mg sodium, 874 mg potassium.

TOMATO-MUSHROOM SOUP

Enjoy this light soup with a toasted cheddar cheese sandwich or a lemony Caesar salad.

1   medium onion, halved, thinly sliced,
        and separated into rings
1   clove garlic, minced
1   tablespoon margarine *or* butter
1   tablespoon olive oil *or* cooking oil
4   cups sliced fresh mushrooms
2½ cups water
¼   cup sweet vermouth *or* dry sherry
¼   cup tomato paste
1   tablespoon instant vegetable,
        chicken, *or* beef bouillon granules
¼   teaspoon pepper
¼   cup finely shredded Parmesan cheese
2   tablespoons snipped parsley *or*
        fresh basil

In a 2-quart saucepan cook onion and garlic in hot margarine or butter and oil about 5 minutes or till onion is tender but not brown. Add mushrooms. Cover and cook about 5 minutes more or till mushrooms are tender. Stir in the water, vermouth or sherry, tomato paste, bouillon granules, and pepper. Bring to a boil; reduce heat. Cover and simmer for 20 minutes.

To serve, ladle soup into individual bowls. Sprinkle with Parmesan cheese and parsley or basil. Makes 4 servings.

Nutrition information per serving: 154 calories, 6 g protein, 11 g carbohydrate, 9 g fat (2 g saturated), 5 mg cholesterol, 1,069 mg sodium, 464 mg potassium.

HEARTY GREEN GUMBO

The "green" in this Cajun-style soup comes from a mixture of spinach, watercress, and parsley. If you don't have watercress, simply increase the parsley to 2 bunches.

1   10-ounce package frozen chopped spinach
1   bunch watercress, chopped (2 cups)
1   bunch parsley, chopped (2 cups)
¼   cup water
½   cup all-purpose flour
½   cup cooking oil
2   large onions, chopped (2 cups)
1   medium green pepper, chopped (1 cup)
2   stalks celery, chopped (1 cup)
    Water
1   teaspoon salt
¼   teaspoon ground red pepper
¼   teaspoon black pepper
1   cup chopped broccoli
1   cup diced parsnips *or* rutabaga
1   15-ounce can cannelini beans, rinsed and drained
2   cups hot cooked rice

In a Dutch oven combine spinach, watercress, parsley, and ¼ cup water. Bring to a boil, breaking up spinach with a fork; reduce heat. Cover and simmer for 10 minutes. Drain, reserving liquid and pressing liquid out with a spatula. Set greens and liquid aside.

In the same Dutch oven stir together the flour and oil till smooth. Cook over medium-high heat for 5 minutes, stirring constantly. Reduce heat to medium. Cook and stir about 10 minutes more or till reddish brown. Add onions, green pepper, and celery. Cook and stir over medium heat for 5 to 10 minutes or till very tender.

Add enough water to reserved liquid to make 2½ cups. Add liquid, cooked greens, salt, red pepper, and black pepper to onion mixture. Bring to a boil; reduce heat. Cover and simmer for 15 minutes. Add broccoli and parsnips or rutabaga. Cover and simmer about 10 minutes more or till tender. Stir in beans; heat through.

To serve, place rice in individual bowls. Ladle gumbo over rice. Makes 6 servings.

Nutrition information per serving: 403 calories, 11 g protein, 53 g carbohydrate, 19 g fat (3 g saturated), 0 mg cholesterol, 548 mg sodium, 763 mg potassium.

SPICY BLACK BEAN CHILI

For a complete meal, serve this spicy chili with fresh-from-the-oven cornbread.

1   cup dry black beans
6   cups water
1   medium onion, chopped (½ cup)
4   cloves garlic, minced
1   tablespoon cooking oil
1   tablespoon chili powder
1   teaspoon ground cumin
1   teaspoon dried oregano, crushed
½   teaspoon paprika
¼   teaspoon salt
¼   teaspoon ground red pepper
4   cups vegetable *or* chicken broth
1   16-ounce can tomatoes, cut up
¼   cup dry sherry *or* water
¼   cup plain low-fat yogurt *or* dairy
      sour cream
1   tablespoon snipped cilantro

Rinse beans. In a large saucepan combine beans and water. Bring to a boil; reduce heat. Simmer for 2 minutes. Remove from heat. Cover and let stand for 1 hour. (Or, skip boiling the water and soak beans overnight in a covered pan.) Drain and rinse beans.

In a large saucepan or Dutch oven cook the onion and garlic in hot oil till tender. Stir in chili powder, cumin, oregano, paprika, salt, and red pepper. Cook and stir for 1 minute. Add the beans, broth, *undrained* tomatoes, and sherry or water. Bring to a boil; reduce heat. Cover and simmer for 1 to 1½ hours or till beans are tender.

To serve, ladle chili into individual bowls. Dollop with yogurt or sour cream and sprinkle with cilantro. Makes 4 servings.

Nutrition information per serving: 231 calories, 11 g protein, 38 g carbohydrate, 6 g fat (1 g saturated), 1 mg cholesterol, 1,432 mg sodium, 752 mg potassium.

ONION-EGGPLANT SOUP PROVENÇALE

This thick soup resembles a stew because its rich broth is chock full of nutty brown rice and tasty vegetables.

2   large onions, thinly sliced and
      separated into rings
2   tablespoons margarine *or* butter
4   cups water
1   small eggplant, peeled and chopped
      (4 cups)
1   small yellow summer squash *or*
      zucchini, thinly sliced (1 cup)
½   cup brown rice
½   of a 6-ounce can (⅓ cup) tomato paste
¼   cup dry red wine
3   vegetable bouillon cubes *or*
      1 tablespoon instant beef
      bouillon granules
1   clove garlic, minced
1½ teaspoons dried basil, crushed
½   teaspoon sugar
¼   teaspoon salt
¼   teaspoon pepper
½   cup orzo *or* other small pasta, cooked
      and drained
4   thin slices French bread, lightly
      toasted
      Olive oil
¼   cup grated Parmesan cheese

In a large saucepan cook the onion in hot margarine or butter till onion is tender but not brown. Carefully add the water, eggplant, squash, brown rice, tomato paste, red wine, bouillon cubes or granules, garlic, basil, sugar, salt, and pepper. Bring to a boil; reduce heat. Cover and simmer for 30 minutes or till vegetables are very tender. Stir in cooked pasta; heat through. Lightly brush each slice of French bread with olive oil.

To serve, ladle the soup into individual bowls. Place one bread slice on top of each serving. Sprinkle with some Parmesan cheese. Makes 4 servings.

Nutrition information per serving: 378 calories, 11 g protein, 55 g carbohydrate, 13 g fat (3 g saturated), 5 mg cholesterol, 1,215 mg sodium, 705 mg potassium.

TORTELLINI-PESTO SOUP WITH VEGETABLES

Pesto is a flavor-packed mixture made from crushing fresh basil, fresh parsley, garlic, grated cheese, nuts, and olive oil. Look for it in your supermarket with fresh pasta or make your own using the recipe on page 139.

1   small onion, chopped (⅓ cup)
2   cloves garlic, minced
1   tablespoon margarine *or* butter
5   cups vegetable *or* chicken broth
2   cups loose-pack frozen mixed
      vegetables
1   9-ounce package fresh cheese-filled
      tortellini
¼   cup purchased pesto *or* Homemade
      Pesto (see recipe, page 139)
¼   cup finely shredded Parmesan cheese

In a large saucepan cook onion and garlic in hot margarine or butter till tender but not brown. Stir in the vegetable or chicken broth and frozen vegetables. Bring to a boil. Stir in tortellini. Return to boiling; reduce heat. Cover and simmer about 8 minutes or till tortellini is al dente (tender but still firm) and vegetables are crisp-tender. Stir in pesto.

To serve, ladle soup into individual bowls. Sprinkle with Parmesan cheese. Makes 4 servings.

Nutrition information per serving: 414 calories, 18 g protein, 51 g carbohydrate, 19 g fat (2 g saturated), 42 mg cholesterol, 1,742 mg sodium, 190 mg potassium.

BARLEY-PUMPKIN SOUP

Compliment the pumpkin flavor in the soup by sprinkling each serving with pumpkin seeds. Look for raw pumpkin seeds at a health food store and toast them on a baking sheet in a 350° oven for 5 to 8 minutes.

4   cups water
1½   cups canned pumpkin *or* mashed
      cooked winter squash
1   medium onion, chopped (½ cup)
⅓   cup quick-cooking barley
4   teaspoons instant vegetable *or*
      chicken bouillon granules
1   clove garlic, minced
½   to 1 teaspoon curry powder
½   teaspoon dried thyme, crushed
1¼   cups milk
¼   cup toasted pumpkin seeds *or*
      sunflower nuts

In a large saucepan combine water, pumpkin or winter squash, onion, barley, bouillon granules, garlic, curry powder, and thyme. Bring to a boil; reduce heat. Cover and simmer for 10 to 15 minutes or till barley is tender. Cool slightly.

Place *half* of the pumpkin mixture in a food processor bowl or blender container. Cover and process or blend till nearly smooth. Pour into a bowl. Repeat with remaining mixture. Return all to saucepan. Stir in milk. Cook and stir over low heat till heated through. *Do not boil.*

To serve, ladle soup into individual bowls. Sprinkle with pumpkin seeds or sunflower nuts. Makes 4 servings.

Nutrition information per serving: 194 calories, 8 g protein, 28 g carbohydrate, 7 g fat (2 g saturated), 6 mg cholesterol, 953 mg sodium, 452 mg potassium.

CHUNKY POTATO-PEPPER SOUP

If you're serving this colorful soup to kids, reduce the ground red pepper to a dash for a milder flavor.

3   medium potatoes, cubed (2¼ cups)
2   cups vegetable *or* chicken broth
1   small green pepper, chopped (½ cup)
1   small red sweet pepper, chopped
      (½ cup)
1   small yellow sweet pepper, chopped
      (½ cup)
1   small onion, chopped (⅓ cup)
¼   cup margarine *or* butter
¼   cup all-purpose flour
¼   teaspoon salt
¼   teaspoon black pepper
⅛   teaspoon ground red pepper
3   cups milk

In a medium saucepan combine potatoes and vegetable or chicken broth. Bring to a boil; reduce heat. Cover and simmer for 10 minutes or till potatoes are tender. *Do not drain.*

Meanwhile, in a large saucepan cook the green pepper, red pepper, yellow pepper, and onion in hot margarine or butter till tender but not brown. Stir in flour, salt, black pepper, and ground red pepper. Add milk all at once. Cook and stir till thickened and bubbly. Cook and stir for 1 minute more. Stir in *undrained* potatoes. Heat through.

To serve, ladle soup into individual bowls. Makes 4 servings.

Nutrition information per serving: 344 calories, 12 g protein, 39 g carbohydrate, 16 g fat (5 g saturated), 14 mg cholesterol, 752 mg sodium, 878 mg potassium.

LENTIL-SPINACH STEW

If you're a spinach lover, you're gonna love this hearty stew. Choose plump-looking lentils and discard any that are shriveled or have spots.

1   cup dry lentils
1   medium onion, chopped (½ cup)
2   cloves garlic, minced
1   tablespoon cooking oil
4   cups water
1   7½-ounce can tomatoes, cut up
4   teaspoons instant vegetable *or* chicken bouillon granules
1   tablespoon Worcestershire sauce
½   teaspoon salt
½   teaspoon dried thyme, crushed
¼   teaspoon fennel seed, crushed
¼   teaspoon pepper
1   bay leaf
2   medium carrots, chopped (1 cup)
1   10-ounce package frozen chopped spinach
1   tablespoon balsamic *or* red wine vinegar

Rinse lentils; set aside. In a large saucepan or Dutch oven cook onion and garlic in hot oil till tender but not brown. Stir in the lentils, water, tomatoes, bouillon granules, Worcestershire sauce, salt, thyme, fennel seed, pepper, and bay leaf. Bring to a boil; reduce heat. Cover and simmer for 20 minutes. Add carrots and frozen spinach. Bring to a boil, breaking up spinach with a fork; reduce heat. Cover and simmer about 15 minutes more or till lentils are tender. Stir in vinegar. Discard bay leaf.

To serve, ladle stew into individual bowls. Makes 4 servings.

Nutrition information per serving: 277 calories, 18 g protein, 45 g carbohydrate, 5 g fat (1 g saturated), 0 mg cholesterol, 1,751 mg sodium, 1,042 mg potassium.

CREAMY TWO-BEAN CHOWDER WITH PESTO

The flavor of pesto really impacts the taste of this chowder. If you're purchasing pesto, choose one with a mild garlic flavor.

8 ounces dry great Northern beans (1 cup)
8 ounces dry pinto beans (1 cup)
6 cups water
4 cups water
2 cups chopped cauliflower
2 medium carrots, shredded (1 cup)
1 medium parsnip, peeled and diced (1 cup)
1 medium leek, chopped (⅓ cup)
1 teaspoon salt
1 teaspoon instant vegetable *or* chicken bouillon granules
1 teaspoon dried oregano, crushed
½ teaspoon dried marjoram, crushed
2 bay leaves
¼ teaspoon pepper
2 cups milk
6 tablespoons purchased pesto *or* Homemade Pesto (see recipe, page 139)

Rinse dry beans. In a Dutch oven combine great Northern beans, pinto beans, and the 6 cups water. Bring to a boil; reduce heat. Simmer for 2 minutes. Remove from heat. Cover and let stand for 1 hour. (Or, skip boiling the water and soak beans overnight in a covered pan.) Drain and rinse beans.

In the Dutch oven combine beans, 4 cups water, cauliflower, carrots, parsnip, leek, salt, bouillon granules, oregano, marjoram, bay leaves, and pepper. Bring to a boil; reduce heat. Cover and simmer for 1½ to 2 hours or till beans are tender, stirring occasionally. Discard bay leaves. Mash beans slightly. Stir in milk and heat through. Season to taste with salt and pepper.

To serve, ladle chowder into individual bowls. Swirl *1 tablespoon* pesto on top of *each* bowl of soup. Makes 6 servings.

Nutrition information per serving: 433 calories, 22 g protein, 60 g carbohydrate, 13 g fat (1 g saturated), 8 mg cholesterol, 683 mg sodium, 1,211 mg potassium.

PEANUT BUTTER-VEGETABLE SOUP

This creamy soup is a sure-fire way to get finicky kids (and adults!) to eat their vegetables.

3 stalks celery, sliced (1½ cups)
2 medium carrots, chopped (1 cup)
1 large onion, chopped (1 cup)
3 cloves garlic, minced
2 tablespoons margarine *or* butter
3 cups water
1 medium potato, diced (1 cup)
1 medium zucchini, sliced (1 cup)
4 teaspoons instant vegetable *or*
    chicken bouillon granules
½ teaspoon pepper
1 16-ounce can tomatoes, cut up
2 tablespoons snipped parsley
½ cup peanut butter

In a large saucepan or Dutch oven cook celery, carrots, onion, and garlic in hot margarine or butter, covered, about 5 minutes or till onion is tender. Stir in water, potato, zucchini, bouillon granules, and pepper. Bring to a boil; reduce heat. Cover and simmer for 10 minutes. Stir in *undrained* tomatoes and parsley.

In a small bowl, gradually stir about *1 cup* broth into peanut butter till smooth. Return mixture to saucepan. Cook and stir till heated through.

To serve, ladle soup into individual bowls. Makes 4 servings.

Nutrition information per serving: 348 calories, 12 g protein, 31 g carbohydrate, 23 g fat (4 g saturated), 0 mg cholesterol, 1,385 mg sodium, 1,007 mg potassium.

VEGETABLE-FAVA BEAN SOUP

Fava beans (also called broad beans) are large, brown, and flat ovals that have an assertive taste and firm texture. They are peeled after briefly cooking them to remove their bitter skins.

1   cup dry fava beans
3   cups water
3   cups water
1   medium carrot, chopped (½ cup)
1   small onion, chopped (⅓ cup)
1   clove garlic, minced
1   tablespoon instant vegetable *or* beef
      bouillon granules
¾   teaspoon dried basil, crushed
1   16-ounce can tomatoes, cut up
1   small zucchini, halved lengthwise and
      sliced (1 cup)
2   ounces linguine *or* spaghetti, broken

Rinse beans. In a large saucepan combine beans and the 3 cups water. Bring to a boil; reduce heat. Simmer, uncovered, for 15 to 30 minutes or till skins soften. Let stand for 1 hour. Drain.

To peel beans, with a knife remove skin from one end of the bean. Peel off remaining skin.

In the same saucepan combine the peeled beans, 3 cups water, carrot, onion, garlic, bouillon granules, and basil. Bring to a boil; reduce heat. Cover and simmer for 40 minutes. Add the *undrained* tomatoes, zucchini, and linguine or spaghetti. Cook, uncovered, for 6 to 8 minutes or till pasta and beans are tender.

To serve, ladle soup into individual bowls. Makes 4 to 6 servings.

Nutrition information per serving: 211 calories, 11 g protein, 41 g carbohydrate, 1 g fat (0 g saturated), 0 mg cholesterol, 895 mg sodium, 687 mg potassium.

SPLIT PEA SOUP WITH SPICED YOGURT

Unlike traditional smooth pea soup, this one is full of chunky vegetables and peas and swirled with a spicy mixture of seasoned yogurt.

1   cup dry split peas
4   cups vegetable *or* chicken broth
¼   teaspoon dried rosemary, crushed
1   bay leaf
1   medium onion, chopped (½ cup)
2   stalks celery, sliced (1 cup)
2   medium carrots, chopped (1 cup)
2   cloves garlic, minced
2   tablespoons dry sherry
½   cup plain low-fat yogurt
¼   teaspoon ground turmeric
¼   teaspoon paprika
¼   teaspoon ground cumin
⅛   teaspoon ground red pepper

Rinse peas. In a large saucepan combine the split peas, vegetable or chicken broth, rosemary, and bay leaf. Bring to a boil; reduce heat. Cover and simmer for 1 hour, stirring occasionally. Stir in the onion, celery, carrots, and garlic. Return to boiling; reduce heat. Cover and simmer for 15 to 20 minutes more or till vegetables are crisp-tender. Discard bay leaf. Stir in sherry.

Meanwhile, in a small bowl stir together the yogurt, turmeric, paprika, cumin, and red pepper.

To serve, ladle soup into individual bowls. Dollop each serving with the spiced yogurt mixture. Makes 4 servings.

Nutrition information per serving: 266 calories, 20 g protein, 40 g carbohydrate, 3 g fat (1 g saturated), 2 mg cholesterol, 852 mg sodium, 967 mg potassium.

TOSSED MEATLESS SALAD NICOISE

Dress up this easy salad with small yellow pear tomatoes when they are in season.

2   medium potatoes, peeled and sliced
      ¼ inch thick
1   9-ounce package frozen cut green
      beans
1   cup cherry tomatoes, halved
1   small yellow *or* green sweet pepper,
      cut into strips
½   cup Greek olives *or* pitted ripe olives
¾   cup bottled Italian salad dressing
4   cups torn romaine lettuce
4   hard-cooked eggs, sliced

In a medium saucepan cook the potatoes in lightly salted boiling water, covered, for 5 minutes. Break up frozen beans and add them to the potatoes in saucepan. Return to boiling; reduce heat. Cover and simmer for 4 to 6 minutes more or till potatoes are tender and green beans are just crisp-tender; drain. Cool slightly.

In a large salad bowl combine potato-green bean mixture, tomatoes, yellow or green peppers, and olives. Pour salad dressing over mixture, tossing gently to coat. Cover and chill for 2 to 3 hours.

To serve, line individual plates with romaine lettuce. Top with vegetable mixture and hard-cooked eggs. Makes 4 servings.

Nutrition information per serving: 410 calories, 11 g protein, 29 g carbohydrate, 30 g fat (5 g saturated), 213 mg cholesterol, 507 mg sodium, 735 mg potassium.

PASTA-MILLET SALAD WITH PORCINI MUSHROOMS

Porcini mushrooms (also called cepe) are wild fungi with large brown caps and thick stems. They add a meaty and somewhat smokey flavor to this lemony pasta salad.

½ cup (½ ounce) dried porcini
    mushrooms
8 cups water
⅓ cup millet
⅔ cup acini di pepe *or* rosamarina
1 cup frozen loose-pack peas
¼ cup salad oil
2 teaspoons finely shredded lemon peel
¼ cup lemon juice
1 clove garlic, minced
½ teaspoon salt
¼ teaspoon paprika
¼ teaspoon pepper
1 large red sweet pepper, chopped
    (1 cup)
1 tablespoon fresh snipped basil *or*
    1 teaspoon dried basil, crushed

Soak dried mushrooms in enough hot water to cover for 15 minutes. Drain. Remove and discard stems. Slice mushrooms. In a large saucepan combine the water, millet, and sliced mushrooms. Bring to a boil; reduce heat. Cook, uncovered, for 10 minutes. Stir in acini di pepe or rosamarina and frozen peas. Return to boiling; reduce heat. Cook, uncovered, for 5 minutes more. Drain in colander. Rinse with cold water. Drain again. Transfer to a large bowl.

For dressing, in a screw-top jar combine salad oil, lemon peel, lemon juice, garlic, salt, paprika, and pepper. Cover and shake well. Pour over millet mixture, tossing to coat. Stir in the chopped red pepper and basil. Cover and chill for 2 to 24 hours, stirring occasionally. Makes 4 servings.

Nutrition information per serving: 358 calories, 9 g protein, 48 g carbohydrate, 15 g fat (2 g saturated), 0 mg cholesterol, 318 mg sodium, 306 mg potassium.

LAYERED TACO SALAD

For a spicier version of this pretty tiered salad, use Monterey Jack cheese with peppers.

1 15-ounce can black beans, rinsed and drained
4 cups shredded iceberg lettuce
1 medium tomato, seeded and chopped
1½ cups shredded cheddar *or* Monterey Jack cheese
¼ cup sliced pitted ripe olives
¼ cup sliced green onion
1 6-ounce carton frozen avocado dip, thawed
½ cup dairy sour cream
1 4-ounce can chopped green chili peppers, drained
1 tablespoon milk
1 clove garlic, minced
½ teaspoon chili powder
   Chopped tomato (optional)
2 cups coarsely crushed tortilla chips

In a 2½-quart glass salad bowl layer black beans, lettuce, tomato, cheese, olives, and onion.

For dressing, in a medium bowl stir together avocado dip, sour cream, chili peppers, milk, garlic, and chili powder. Spread over the top of the salad. If desired, sprinkle with chopped tomato. Cover the surface with plastic wrap and chill for 2 to 24 hours.

Before serving, toss salad together and serve over crushed tortilla chips. Makes 4 servings.

Nutrition information per serving: 561 calories, 24 g protein, 37 g carbohydrate, 40 g fat (14 g saturated), 58 mg cholesterol, 1,277 mg sodium, 794 mg potassium.

MINTED TOMATO TABBOULEH SALAD

Taboubouleh (tuh-BOO-luh) is to the Middle East what potato salad is to the United States. The mainstay of this refreshing salad is bulgur, also known as precooked cracked wheat. You can find bulgur at large supermarkets or health food stores.

1 cup bulgur
1½ cups boiling water
2 14-ounce cans stewed tomatoes
1 cup snipped parsley
½ cup snipped fresh mint
½ cup currants *or* raisins
½ cup olive oil *or* salad oil
⅓ cup lemon juice
2 cloves garlic, minced
2 teaspoons curry powder
½ teaspoon ground cumin
¼ teaspoon ground cinnamon
3 cups shredded lettuce
½ cup peanuts

In a colander rinse bulgur with cold water; drain well. Transfer bulgur to a small bowl. Pour boiling water over bulgur. Let stand 15 minutes. Drain well.

Drain tomatoes, reserving *½ cup* juices. Cut up any large tomato pieces. In a large bowl stir together drained tomatoes, parsley, mint and currants or raisins. Toss bulgur with tomato mixture.

For dressing, in a small food processor bowl or blender container combine reserved tomato juice, oil, lemon juice, garlic, curry powder, cumin, and cinnamon. Cover and process or blend till smooth. Pour over bulgur mixture; toss to coat. Cover and chill for 4 to 24 hours (liquid is absorbed during chilling).

To serve, line individual plates with shredded lettuce. Spoon bulgur mixture over lettuce. Sprinkle with peanuts. Makes 4 servings.

Nutrition information per serving: 617 calories, 13 g protein, 64 g carbohydrate, 38 g fat (5 g saturated), 0 mg cholesterol, 792 mg sodium, 1,078 mg potassium.

SIZZLING GOAT CHEESE SALAD

We call this a sizzling salad because tender disks of goat cheese are coated with a crumb mixture and cooked till they are crispy and sizzling. Then the warm cheese is tossed with a mixture of seasonal greens and drizzled with an easy vinaigrette dressing.

4 cups torn mixed greens
½ cup pitted ripe olives
6 whole dried tomatoes in oil, drained and chopped *or* 6 whole dried tomatoes, rehydrated according to package directions, drained, and chopped
2 teaspoons sliced green onion
¼ cup salad oil
¼ cup tarragon vinegar
2 tablespoons water
1 tablespoon walnut oil *or* salad oil
1 tablespoon Dijon-style mustard
1 egg
1 tablespoon water
2 tablespoons cornmeal
1 tablespoon fine dry bread crumbs
1 tablespoon sesame seed, toasted
1 tablespoon grated Parmesan cheese
8 ounces chèvre (goat's cheese)
2 tablespoons margarine *or* butter
4 small pita bread rounds, split horizontally, cut into wedges, and toasted

On a serving platter arrange greens, olives, tomatoes, and green onions. Cover and chill.

For dressing, in a screw-top jar combine salad oil, vinegar, 2 tablespoons water, walnut or salad oil, and mustard. Cover and shake till well combined. Chill.

In a small bowl combine egg and 1 tablespoon water. In a shallow bowl combine cornmeal, bread crumbs, sesame seed, and Parmesan cheese. Divide chèvre into 16 equal portions; shape into balls and flatten into 1¼-inch diameter patties. Dip each patty into the egg mixture; coat with cornmeal mixture. Cover and chill.

At serving time, in a large skillet melt margarine or butter. Add cheese patties and cook over medium heat for 3 to 5 minutes or till golden, turning once. Arrange on top of greens mixture. Shake dressing and drizzle over greens mixture and cheese. Serve with pita bread wedges. Makes 4 servings.

Nutrition information per serving: 539 calories, 19 g protein, 25 g carbohydrate, 42 g fat (13 g saturated), 80 mg cholesterol, 688 mg sodium, 342 mg potassium.

GREEK-STYLE LENTIL SALAD

Lentils are a member of the legume family and provide an excellent source of vegetable protein. Cooked lentils have a beanlike texture and a mild, nutty flavor. You can store lentils, tightly wrapped, in a cool, dry place for up to 1 year.

1½ cups water
¾ cup bulgur
¼ teaspoon salt
¾ cup dry lentils
2 cups water
1 medium tomato, cut into thin wedges
1 small cucumber, quartered lengthwise
    and sliced
¼ cup chopped red *or* white onion
1 2¼-ounce can sliced pitted ripe
    olives, drained
    Greek-Style Vinaigrette
½ cup crumbled feta *or* blue cheese
    (2 ounces)

In a medium saucepan bring 1½ cups water to a boil; remove from heat. Stir in bulgur and salt. Cover; let stand for 30 minutes. Drain thoroughly, pressing bulgur to remove excess water.

Meanwhile, rinse lentils. In another medium saucepan combine 2 cups water and the lentils. Bring to a boil; reduce heat. Cover and simmer for 20 minutes or till tender; drain. Rinse with cold water; drain again.

In a large mixing bowl combine cooked bulgur, cooked lentils, tomato, cucumber, onion, and olives. Toss mixture with Greek-Style Vinaigrette. Cover and chill at least 4 hours or overnight. Before serving, stir in feta or blue cheese. Makes 4 servings.

Greek-Style Vinaigrette: In a screw-top jar combine ⅓ cup *olive oil or salad oil*, 3 tablespoons *red wine vinegar*, 1 tablespoon *sugar*, 1 tablespoon *lemon juice*, 1 teaspoon *Dijon-style mustard*, and ½ teaspoon *dried oregano*, crushed. Cover and shake well. Cover and store in the refrigerator for up to 2 weeks. Shake before using. Makes about ½ cup.

Nutrition information per serving: 478 calories, 17 g protein, 55 g carbohydrate, 24 g fat (5 g saturated), 12 mg cholesterol, 768 mg sodium, 762 mg potassium.

WHEAT BERRY-WALNUT SALAD IN PAPAYA SHELLS

Wheat berries (unpolished whole wheat kernels) give this salad a delicious high-fiber boost. You can use either hard or soft wheat berries which are available at health food stores.

2   cups water
⅔   cup wheat berries
2   papayas
1   cup strawberries, halved
1   stalk celery, sliced (½ cup)
½   cup vanilla yogurt
2   tablespoons mayonnaise *or* salad
     dressing
¼   teaspoon ground ginger
     Lettuce leaves
½   cup coarsely chopped walnuts,
     toasted

In a small saucepan combine water and wheat berries. Bring to a boil; reduce heat. Cover and simmer about 1 hour or till wheat berries are tender. Drain and cool.

For papaya shells, use a sharp knife to cut the papayas lengthwise in half. Remove seeds. Cut out papaya pulp, leaving ¼-inch thick shells. Cover and chill shells. Cut papaya pulp into ½-inch cubes.

In a large mixing bowl combine papaya cubes, cooked wheat berries, strawberries, and celery. For dressing, in a small bowl stir together the yogurt, mayonnaise or salad dressing, and ginger. Pour over wheat berry mixture, tossing gently to coat. If desired, cover and chill for up to 4 hours.

To serve, place papaya shells on individual lettuce-lined plates. Spoon wheat berry mixture into papaya shells. Sprinkle with walnuts. Makes 4 servings.

Nutrition information per serving: 324 calories, 8 g protein, 42 g carbohydrate, 16 g fat (2 g saturated), 6 mg cholesterol, 79 mg sodium, 533 mg potassium.

TOFU-DRESSED VEGETARIAN SALAD

Tangy blue cheese is prevalent in every bite of this meal-sized salad. You can substitute 4 ounces of any other crumbly cheese (like feta or goat's milk) or shredded hard cheese.

½ cup mayonnaise *or* salad dressing
4 ounces tofu (fresh bean curd)
½ teaspoon fines herbes, crushed
1 to 2 tablespoons milk
5 cups torn romaine lettuce
1 cup torn radicchio
1 cup chopped enoki mushrooms *or* sliced button mushrooms
1 medium yellow *or* green sweet pepper, chopped
4 ounces blue cheese, crumbled (1 cup)
½ cup coarsely chopped pecans, toasted
¼ cup chopped shallots

For dressing, in a food processor bowl or blender container combine the mayonnaise or salad dressing, tofu, and fines herbes. Cover and process or blend till smooth. If necessary, stir in some milk.

Arrange the romaine, radicchio, mushrooms, pepper, blue cheese, pecans, and shallots on individual plates. Serve dressing alongside. Makes 4 servings.

Note: For fancy pepper shapes, use a star, moon, heart, or other shape of aspic cutter or hors d'oeuvre cutter to cut shapes from strips of yellow or green sweet pepper.

Nutrition information per serving: 509 calories, 12 g protein, 11 g carbohydrate, 48 g fat (11 g saturated), 43 mg cholesterol, 617 mg sodium, 553 mg potassium.

SOUTHWEST BEAN SALAD WITH LIME VINAIGRETTE

Kidney beans, garbanzo beans, crunchy vegetables, and cheese are marinated in a fresh-tasting lime dressing and served over lettuce. Go ahead and choose any combination of canned beans that you like.

1   15-ounce can red kidney beans, rinsed and drained
1   15-ounce can garbanzo beans, rinsed and drained
1   small zucchini *or* yellow summer squash, thinly sliced
2   small carrots, cut into julienne strips
1   small red onion, sliced and separated into rings
4   ounces Monterey Jack cheese with jalapeño peppers, cubed (1 cup)
¼   cup olive oil *or* salad oil
1   teaspoon finely shredded lime peel
¼   cup lime juice
1   to 2 tablespoons snipped cilantro *or* parsley
1   tablespoon water
1   clove garlic, minced
¼   teaspoon salt
¼   teaspoon ground cumin
¼   teaspoon ground cardamom
    Lettuce leaves

In a large mixing bowl combine the kidney beans, garbanzo beans, zucchini or yellow squash, carrots, onion, and cheese.

For dressing, in a screw-top jar combine the olive oil or salad oil, lime peel, lime juice, cilantro or parsley, water, garlic, salt, cumin, and cardamom. Cover and shake well. Pour the dressing over the bean mixture, tossing to coat. Cover and chill for 2 to 24 hours, stirring occasionally.

To serve, use a slotted spoon to spoon salad onto individual lettuce-lined plates or bowls. Makes 4 servings.

Nutrition information per serving: 448 calories, 21 g protein, 44 g carbohydrate, 25 g fat (8 g saturated), 25 mg cholesterol, 908 mg sodium, 658 mg potassium.

ORIENTAL SPECKLED RICE SALAD

The Oriental flavor of this salad comes from a tasty mixture of teriyaki sauce, rice wine vinegar, sesame oil, and crushed red pepper. Serve it with a crusty loaf of bread.

⅛ cup wild rice
⅛ cup brown rice
1½ cups water
3 tablespoons teriyaki sauce
2 tablespoons rice wine vinegar
2 teaspoons toasted sesame oil
2 teaspoons honey
¼ teaspoon crushed red pepper
⅓ cup shredded carrot
1 6-ounce package frozen pea pods, thawed, drained, and halved diagonally
½ cup peanuts, coarsely chopped

Place wild rice in a colander and rinse under cold water. In a medium saucepan bring wild rice, brown rice, and water to a boil; reduce heat. Cover and simmer for 45 to 50 minutes or till water is absorbed and rice is tender. Remove from heat.

For dressing, in a screw-top jar combine the teriyaki sauce, rice wine vinegar, sesame oil, honey, and crushed red pepper. Cover and shake the dressing well.

Transfer the rice mixture to a bowl. Stir in the shredded carrot. Pour the dressing mixture over rice mixture, tossing to coat. Cover and chill for 2 to 24 hours.

Before serving, toss the rice mixture with the pea pods and peanuts. Makes 4 servings.

Nutrition information per serving: 277 calories, 10 g protein, 35 g carbohydrate, 12 g fat (7 g saturated), 0 mg cholesterol, 530 mg sodium, 375 mg potassium.

SUPER SALAD PIZZA

Choose the "greens" of your liking from a selection of spinach, romaine, radicchio, arugula, watercress, romaine, Bibb lettuce, or Boston lettuce.

½ of a 17¼-ounce package (1 sheet) frozen puff pastry, thawed
3   cups torn mixed greens
½ of a 9-ounce package frozen artichoke hearts, thawed, drained, and quartered
6   cherry tomatoes, halved
1   4-ounce container (½ cup) semisoft cheese with garlic and herbs *or* ½ cup soft-style cream cheese with chives and onion
2   teaspoons Dijon-style mustard
1   to 2 tablespoons milk
2   cups shredded mozzarella cheese (8 ounces)
½ of a medium avocado, peeled and sliced

On a lightly floured surface roll pastry into a 12-inch square; cut into a 12-inch circle. Place pastry on a 12-inch pizza pan or large baking sheet. Use a fork to generously prick pastry. Bake in a 375° oven for 15 to 18 minutes or till golden (pastry will shrink). Cool.

Meanwhile, in a large mixing bowl combine the greens, artichoke hearts, and tomatoes.

For dressing, in a small bowl stir together the semisoft or soft-style cream cheese, mustard, and enough milk to make of drizzling consistency. Drizzle *half* of the dressing over the greens mixture, tossing to coat.

Preheat the broiler. Sprinkle *1½ cups* of the mozzarella cheese evenly over the crust. Broil 3 inches from the heat for 1 to 1½ minutes or till the cheese melts. Spoon greens mixture evenly over melted cheese. Sprinkle with remaining mozzarella cheese. Broil 3 inches from the heat for 1 to 2 minutes more or till cheese melts. Arrange avocado slices on top. Cut into wedges. Serve at once with remaining dressing. Makes 6 servings.

Nutrition information per serving: 389 calories, 14 g protein, 21 g carbohydrate, 28 g fat (8 g saturated), 42 mg cholesterol, 462 mg sodium, 395 mg potassium.

ASPARAGUS EGG SALAD WITH DILL DRESSING

Serve this knife-and-fork sandwich on your favorite toasted bagel or English muffin halves.

8 ounces fresh asparagus, cut into 1-inch pieces *or* 1 cup small broccoli flowerets
8 hard-cooked eggs, chopped
2 green onions, finely chopped (¼ cup)
2 tablespoons diced pimiento
¼ cup mayonnaise *or* salad dressing
1 teaspoon snipped fresh dill *or* ¼ teaspoon dried dillweed
1 teaspoon Dijon-style mustard
½ teaspoon white wine vinegar *or* lemon juice
¼ teaspoon salt
⅛ teaspoon pepper
 Alfalfa sprouts
4 bagels *or* English muffins, split and toasted

In a small saucepan cook asparagus or small broccoli flowerets in a small amount of boiling water for 3 minutes; drain and rinse under cold water. Drain well.

In a large mixing bowl combine the asparagus or broccoli, eggs, green onions, and pimiento.

For dressing, in a small mixing bowl stir together the mayonnaise or salad dressing, dill or dillweed, mustard, and vinegar or lemon juice. Stir dressing into egg mixture. Add salt and pepper to taste.

Arrange alfalfa sprouts on bagel or muffin halves. Spoon egg mixture over sprouts. Makes 4 servings.

Nutrition information per serving: 335 calories, 20 g protein, 34 g carbohydrate, 13 g fat (4 g saturated), 427 mg cholesterol, 494 mg sodium, 273 mg potassium.

TOFU SALAD SANDWICHES

This egg salad look-a-like is loaded with fresh and dried fruit, crunchy celery, and toasted almonds with a light curry dressing. It feels equally at home as a sandwich filling or a salad.

1   10½-ounce package extra-firm tofu
     (fresh bean curd)
1   cup seedless green grapes, halved
¼   cup sliced celery
¼   cup slivered almonds, toasted
¼   cup raisins
½   cup mayonnaise *or* salad dressing
½   teaspoon curry powder
¼   teaspoon salt
¼   teaspoon ground ginger
     Lettuce leaves
     Whole grain toast

If necessary, drain tofu; discard liquid. Finely chop tofu. In a large bowl combine chopped tofu, grapes, celery, almonds, and raisins.

For dressing, stir together the mayonnaise or salad dressing, curry powder, salt, and ginger. Add dressing to tofu mixture, stirring to combine. Cover and chill till serving time (2 to 24 hours).

To serve, spread the tofu mixture on lettuce-lined toast. Makes 4 servings.

Nutrition information per serving: 465 calories, 15 g protein, 33 g carbohydrate, 33 g fat (4 g saturated), 16 mg cholesterol, 618 mg sodium, 468 mg potassium.

GRILLED BRIE SANDWICHES WITH GREENS AND GARLIC

Instead of using all spinach for this deluxe grilled cheese sandwich, try a combination of half watercress and half spinach.

2   cloves garlic, minced
1   tablespoon olive oil *or* cooking oil
8   ounces fresh spinach, rinsed and
        stemmed (6 cups)
8   ounces cold Brie, cut into ⅛-inch
        slices
8   slices firm-textured whole grain bread
     Margarine *or* butter

In a large skillet cook garlic in hot oil for 30 seconds. Add spinach. Cook over medium heat, tossing till spinach begins to wilt; remove from heat. Set aside.

Divide the cheese among *4 slices* of the bread. Top with spinach-garlic mixture. Cover with remaining bread slices. Lightly butter the outside of each sandwich.

In a large skillet cook *half* of the sandwiches over medium-low heat for 5 to 7 minutes or till golden brown. Turn sandwich and cook for 2 minutes more or till golden brown and cheese melts. Transfer to a warm oven. Repeat with remaining sandwiches. Makes 4 servings.

Nutrition information per serving: 405 calories, 18 g protein, 25 g carbohydrate, 27 g fat (12 g saturated), 57 mg cholesterol, 771 mg sodium, 381 mg potassium.

CHEESE AND VEGGIE SANDWICHES

If you're watching your sodium intake, you can reduce the salt in cottage cheese by placing it in a colander and rinsing under cold water.

1½ cups cottage cheese, drained
¼ cup shredded carrot
¼ cup chopped green pepper *or* celery
½ teaspoon finely snipped chives
¼ cup plain low-fat yogurt
8 small slices whole grain bread
2 tablespoons horseradish mustard
   Spinach *or* lettuce leaves
4 tomato slices

In a medium mixing bowl combine the cottage cheese, carrot, green pepper or celery, and chives. Stir in the yogurt.

Spread the bread slices with horseradish mustard; top with spinach or lettuce leaves. Spoon the cheese mixture onto *half* of the bread slices. Top with a tomato slice and remaining bread slices. Makes 4 servings.

Nutrition information per serving: 232 calories, 16 g protein, 29 g carbohydrate, 7 g fat (3 g saturated), 13 mg cholesterol, 722 mg sodium, 316 mg potassium.

SPINACH-GRÛYÉRE CALZONES

Calzones are like closed-face pizzas because the cheesy filling is encased in a crisp bundle of dough. These are especially easy to make thanks to refrigerated pizza dough.

1   10-ounce package frozen chopped
    spinach
1½ cups shredded Grûyére *or* Swiss
    cheese (6 ounces)
½   cup ricotta cheese
1   green onion, thinly sliced
    (2 tablespoons)
½   teaspoon dried basil, crushed
¼   teaspoon garlic powder
¼   teaspoon pepper
1   10-ounce package refrigerated pizza
    dough
    Water
1   egg
1   teaspoon water
¼   cup grated Parmesan cheese

Cook spinach according to package directions; drain well. In a large mixing bowl stir together the spinach, Grûyére or Swiss cheese, ricotta cheese, green onion, basil, garlic powder, and pepper. Unroll pizza dough. Roll or stretch dough into a 15x10-inch rectangle. Cut into six 5-inch squares. Divide spinach mixture among squares. Brush edges with water. Lift one corner and stretch dough over to the opposite corner. Press edges of the dough well with a fork to seal.

Arrange calzones on a greased baking sheet. Prick tops with a fork. Combine the egg and 1 teaspoon water; brush over calzones. Sprinkle with the Parmesan cheese. Bake in a 425° oven about 10 minutes or till golden brown. Let stand for 5 minutes before serving. Makes 6 servings.

Nutrition information per serving: 366 calories, 20 g protein, 35 g carbohydrate, 16 g fat (8 g saturated), 76 mg cholesterol, 518 mg sodium, 278 mg potassium.

GARBANZO BEAN SPREAD (HUMMUS)

If you can't find tahini at your local health food store, make an easy substitute by stirring together ¼ cup peanut butter and 1 teaspoon toasted sesame oil till well combined.

1   15-ounce can garbanzo beans, rinsed
    and drained
¼   cup tahini (sesame seed paste)
¼   cup lemon juice
1   tablespoon olive oil *or* salad oil
2   cloves garlic, quartered
½   teaspoon salt
¼   teaspoon paprika
½   cup snipped parsley
1   2-ounce jar diced pimiento, drained
    (¼ cup)
5   pita bread rounds

In a food processor bowl or blender container combine beans, tahini, lemon juice, oil, garlic, salt, and paprika. Cover and process or blend till smooth, stopping and scraping sides as necessary. Transfer to a bowl. Stir in parsley and pimiento. Cover and chill 2 to 24 hours.

To serve, split pita rounds horizontally and cut into wedges. Broil 4 to 5 inches from the heat about 1 minute or till light brown and crisp. Serve with spread. Makes about 1⅔ cups spread or 5 servings.

Nutrition information per serving: 298 calories, 12 g protein, 38 g carbohydrate, 12 g fat (1 g saturated), 0 mg cholesterol, 776 mg sodium, 334 mg potassium.

OPEN-FACED DRIED TOMATO MELT

Dried tomatoes start out as ripe Roma tomatoes that are salted and heat-dried or sun-dried. The result is a chewy, meaty tomato with a concentrated flavor.

¼   cup Homemade Pesto (see recipe, at
       right) *or* purchased pesto
2   tablespoons chopped nuts
4   1-inch thick slices sourdough French
       bread, toasted
¼   cup dried tomatoes in oil, drained
       and chopped
1   cup shredded mozzarella cheese
       (4 ounces)

In a small bowl stir together pesto and nuts. Spread pesto mixture over French bread slices. Top with dried tomatoes and mozzarella cheese. Place on a baking sheet. Broil about 4 inches from the heat for 2 to 3 minutes or till cheese melts. Makes 2 servings.

Nutrition information per serving: 587 calories, 25 g protein, 44 g carbohydrate, 34 g fat (6 g saturated), 36 mg cholesterol, 918 mg sodium, 323 mg potassium.

Homemade Pesto: In a blender container or food processor bowl combine 1 cup firmly packed *fresh basil leaves;* ½ cup firmly packed *parsley sprigs with stems removed;* ½ cup grated *Parmesan or Romano cheese;* ¼ cup *pine nuts, walnuts, or almonds;* 1 large cloved *garlic, quartered;* and ¼ teaspoon *salt.* Cover and blend or process with several on-off turns till a paste forms, stopping the machine several times and scraping the sides.

With the machine running slowly, gradually add ¼ cup *olive oil or cooking oil* and blend or process to the consistency of soft butter. Divide into 3 portions (about ¼ cup each) and place in small airtight containers. Refrigerate for 1 or 2 days or freeze up to 1 month.

To serve, thaw 1 portion pesto, if frozen. Bring to room temperature.

FRUIT AND CHEESE POCKETS

This refreshing pita sandwich doubles easily to serve four hungry lunch eaters.

½ cup cottage cheese
½ cup diced sharp cheddar *or* Swiss
    cheese (2 ounces)
1 kiwifruit, peeled and quartered
    and/*or* ½ cup sliced strawberries
¼ cup drained pineapple tidbits
1 tablespoon snipped fresh chives *or*
    finely chopped green onion
    (green part only)
    Lettuce leaves
1 large pita bread round, split crosswise

In a small bowl stir together cottage cheese, cheddar or Swiss cheese, kiwifruit or strawberries, pineapple tidbits, and chives or onion.

To serve, place lettuce leaves in pita halves. Spoon the fruit and cheese mixture into pitas. Makes 2 servings.

Nutrition information per serving: 265 calories, 16 g protein, 23 g carbohydrate, 12 g fat (7 g saturated), 38 mg cholesterol, 499 mg sodium, 302 mg potassium.

Keep track of your daily nutrition needs by using the information we provide at the end of each recipe. We've analyzed the nutritional content of each recipe serving for you. When a recipe gives an ingredient substitution, we used the first choice in the analysis. If it makes a range of servings (such as 4 to 6), we used the smallest number. Ingredients listed as optional weren't included in the calculations.

METRIC COOKING HINTS

By making a few conversions, cooks in Australia, Canada, and the United Kingdom can use the recipes in Better Homes and Gardens® *Vegetarian Recipes* with confidence. The charts on this page provide a guide for converting measurements from the U.S. customary system, which is used throughout this book, to the imperial and metric systems. There also is a conversion table for oven temperatures to accommodate the differences in oven calibrations.

Volume and Weight: Americans traditionally use cup measures for liquid and solid ingredients. The chart (top right) shows the approximate imperial and metric equivalents. If you are accustomed to weighing solid ingredients, here are some helpful approximate equivalents.

■ 1 cup butter, caster sugar, or rice = 8 ounces = about 250 grams
■ 1 cup flour = 4 ounces = about 125 grams
■ 1 cup icing sugar = 5 ounces = about 150 grams
   Spoon measures are used for smaller amounts of ingredients. Although the size of the tablespoon varies slightly among countries. However, for practical purposes and for recipes in this book, a straight substitution is all that's necessary.

   Measurements made using cups or spoons should always be level, unless stated otherwise.

Product Differences: Most of the ingredients called for in the recipes in this book are available in English-speaking countries. However, some are known by different names. Here are some common American ingredients and their possible counterparts:
■ Sugar is granulated or caster sugar.
■ Powdered sugar is icing sugar.
■ All-purpose flour is plain household flour or white flour. When self-rising flour is used in place of all-purpose flour in a recipe that calls for leavening, omit the leavening agent (baking soda or baking powder) and salt.
■ Light corn syrup is golden syrup.
■ Cornstarch is cornflour.
■ Baking soda is bicarbonate of soda.
■ Vanilla is vanilla essence.

USEFUL EQUIVALENTS

⅛ teaspoon = 0.5ml
¼ teaspoon = 1ml
½ teaspoon = 2 ml
1 teaspoon = 5 ml
¼ cup = 2 fluid ounces = 50ml
⅓ cup = 3 fluid ounces = 75ml
½ cup = 4 fluid ounces = 125ml

⅔ cup = 5 fluid ounces = 150ml
¾ cup = 6 fluid ounces = 175ml
1 cup = 8 fluid ounces = 250ml
2 cups = 1 pint
2 pints = 1 litre
½ inch =1 centimetre
1 inch = 2 centimetres

BAKING PAN SIZES

American	Metric
8x1½-inch round baking pan	20x4-centimetre sandwich or cake tin
9x1½-inch round baking pan	23x3.5-centimetre sandwich or cake tin
11x7x1½-inch baking pan	28x18x4-centimetre baking pan
13x9x2-inch baking pan	32.5x23x5-centimetre baking pan
2-quart rectangular baking dish	30x19x5-centimetre baking pan
15x10x1-inch baking pan	38x25.5x2.5-centimetre baking pan (Swiss roll tin)
9-inch pie plate	22x4- or 23x4-centimetre pie plate
7- or 8-inch springform pan	18- or 20-centimetre springform or loose-bottom cake tin
9x5x3-inch loaf pan	23x13x6-centimetre or 2-pound narrow loaf pan or paté tin
1½-quart casserole	1.5-litre casserole
2-quart casserole	2-litre casserole

OVEN TEMPERATURE EQUIVALENTS

Fahrenheit Setting	Celsius Setting*	Gas Setting
300°F	150°C	Gas Mark 2
325°F	160°C	Gas Mark 3
350°F	180°C	Gas Mark 4
375°F	190°C	Gas Mark 5
400°F	200°C	Gas Mark 6
425°F	220°C	Gas Mark 7
450°F	230°C	Gas Mark 8
Broil		Grill

*Electric and gas ovens may be calibrated using Celsius. However, increase the Celsius setting 10 to 20 degrees when cooking above 160°C with an electric oven. For convection or forced-air ovens (gas or electric), lower the temperature setting 10°C when cooking at all heat levels.